THE LEAVING HOME SURVIVAL GUIDE

Nicola Morgan was born and brought up in a boys' boarding school, where her parents both taught. She studied classics and philosophy at Cambridge University, before going on to become a teacher herself and specializing in literacy. But Nicola's ambition was to be an author, and she has now written around seventy home-learning titles, as well as a series of Thomas the Tank Engine stories and several critically acclaimed novels for teens. Her novels *Fleshmarket* and *Sleepwalking* each won a Scottish Arts Council Award. Nicola is also the author of *Chicken Friend* and *Blame My Brain*, both published by Walker Books. She lives in Edinburgh with her husband and two daughters.

Books by the same author

Blame My Brain: The Amazing Teenage Brain Revealed
Chicken Friend

First published 2005 by Walker Books Ltd
87 Vauxhall Walk, London SE11 5HJ

2 4 6 8 10 9 7 5 3 1

© 2005 Nicola Morgan

The right of Nicola Morgan to be identified as author of this work
has been asserted by her in accordance with the
Copyright, Designs and Patents Act 1988

This book has been typeset in Sabon, Caecilia and Myriad

Printed and bound in Great Britain by William Clowes Ltd, Beccles, Suffolk

British Library Cataloguing in Publication Data:
a catalogue record for this book
is available from the British Library

ISBN 1-84428-771-8

www.walkerbooks.co.uk

Enjoy the freedom!
Nicola Morgan

NICOLA MORGAN

THE LEAVING HOME SURVIVAL GUIDE

WALKER BOOKS

AND SUBSIDIARIES

LONDON · BOSTON · SYDNEY · AUCKLAND

To my daughters, Hannah and Rebecca:
if you read this, I promise not to nag.
Too often.

Acknowledgements

Huge thanks for expert advice from Dr Murray Fisken,
Johnny Ballantine CA, Jackie Jackson and Mark Bennett;
and to all the lovely people at Walker Books, especially:
Caroline Royds and Emil Fortune for deeply intelligent editing,
Patrick Insole for the great cover, and Chris Kloet for getting
me started in the first place.

Contents

Introduction 7

How to use this book 9

1. Your money 11

2. Accommodation 61

3. In the home 89

4. Food matters 143

5. Health 181

6. Work and study 233

7. Keeping yourself safe 247

8. The law and you 263

9. Emergencies 281

Index 323

Introduction

So, you're leaving home? Freedom is doing more than beckoning – it's yelling 'Party-time!' in your ear. No more rules. No more nagging adults telling you to tidy your room or eat your greens or come home before dawn. No more being treated like a child.

Excellent!

You're on your own.

No more meals cooked for you. No more washing miraculously appearing ironed and folded. No more fridges full of tasty and expensive food. Did you know it was expensive? No more bills paid for you.

Not so excellent.

It's all going wrong. Your white t-shirts are a weak shade of slate and suddenly too small because you didn't understand the washing symbols. There's a red wine stain in the middle of the carpet because you don't know how to get rid of it. Last week you had food poisoning because you didn't know that reheating food is risky if you don't do it properly. And what is the correct temperature for a fridge anyway? Your landlord is refusing to repair a broken window and you don't know your rights. There's a smell coming from the kitchen sink and the water seems to be going down far too slowly. You are sick of pot noodles and tinned soup and you know that ready-meals are expensive and bad for you but you haven't a clue how to cook. You keep getting colds and you don't know why. You can't find a doctor who will let you register.

You're on your own. Your kettle stops working. You phone home. 'Maybe it's a fuse,' says your mum. What the hell's a fuse? Your bike gets stolen. 'Don't worry,' says your dad. 'Your insurance will cover it.' You did pay your insurance premium, didn't you? You are freezing cold but you don't know how much it will cost to put the electric heater on for a few minutes and the last electricity bill was horrendous. Suddenly, there's a hissing sound. You leap to your feet and rush through to where it seems to be coming from. Water is spraying out of a burst pipe under the bathroom sink.

You phone home. 'Dad, there's water spraying from a pipe under the sink,' you shriek.

'Which sink?' he asks, calmly.

Does it MATTER? 'Bathroom.'

'Is there an isolating valve?'

'What!?'

'Well, just turn off the mains then.'

'What the hell is the mains?'

Yes, this is just a bad dream. This isn't going to happen to you, because you have *The Leaving Home Survival Guide*. It will tell you how to deal with all these situations and more – and better still, prevent them happening in the first place. Best of all, you won't have to phone home with a desperate, plaintive voice and ask for help, so your parents will never, ever have the chance to be smug. 'I told you so,' won't even get a look in.

Don't leave home without it.

How to use this book

Obviously you know how to use a book, but this one has some special features.

> ➤ **Read it** – OK, not such a special feature.
>
> ➤ **In an emergency, use the emergency section** – there's a black strip down the edge of this section so you can find it even if you are in a blind panic.
>
> ➤ **Troubleshoot** – well, no book can contain everything so you may want further help. Or you may want specific information about a particular bank or product or company or organization, or something local to you. The Troubleshoot sections are at the end of every chapter. They tell you where to go for all the things I didn't have room to tell you. Or forgot.
>
> ➤ **Add to it** – at the end of the book is space for you to write information that you find yourself. Or things like your NHS medical number, GP's phone number, landlord's phone number, location of the water mains…

Your money

Contents

Introduction 15

Bank accounts 16
How to choose a bank 16
Internet banking? 19
Ethical banking? 20

Bank charges 21

Your bank statement
. 22
Writing a cheque 22

**Building society
accounts** 24

Interest 25
APR 25
Gross or net? 26

Saving 27
National Savings account 27

Debit cards 28

**Credit cards
(and store cards)** 29
Affinity cards 31
Credit cashback cards 31

Other things to know about
credit cards 31
0% credit? 32
Card protection and fraud 33
How to minimize the risk
of fraud 34

**Direct debits and
standing orders** 36
The difference between
direct debits and standing
orders 36

Paying bills 38

Credit rating 39
Checking or changing your
credit rating 39

**Tax and National
Insurance** 42
Evasion or avoidance 43
What is a tax return? 43

Insurance 45
Contents/possessions
insurance 46
Car insurance 48
Travel insurance 48

Extended warranties 49

Budgeting 51
Cutting expenses 52
Cutting electricity bills 53
Cutting gas bills 54
Debt problems 54

Scams 56
Signs that should make you
    suspicious 56

Benefits 58

Summary 58

Troubleshoot 59

1

YOUR MONEY

1

YOUR MONEY

Introduction

Cash, dosh, readies, lolly, filthy lucre – whatever you call it, you probably think you don't have enough of it. What's even more certain is that if you don't know how to look after it, you're soon going to have a lot less of it. Once you are 18, you are legally responsible for all your debts and your parents do not have to help you out if you can't pay a bill. Time to start being extremely nice to them, I'd say.

Not having enough money is an important part of being young. It's character-building. Easy for me to say, since I'm not young any more. But seriously, if you don't suffer a bit now and spend some time re-using tea bags and counting out grains of rice, how will you ever say to your own children or nephews and nieces, 'Ah, when I was young, I suffered – oh, how I suffered! You young people today, you just don't know you're born. Holidays to the moon, parties in Timbuktoo – I mean, in *my* day I only had one television in my bedroom and now you've got one in each wall.'

So, look after what you've got and look forward to the day when, through your own hard work (and rather a lot of luck), you can celebrate with lobster and champagne in the most expensive restaurant. Meanwhile, enjoy the pain.

Bank accounts

You need one. But which bank? And which account? You may already have a bank account, but once you are 18 you will need a different one. You need more flexibility than when you were 12. You need to be able to get your money out straight away and easily. You will also want a chequebook with guarantee card, which you weren't allowed before you were 18. Your guarantee card will usually also be a Maestro or Delta card, which gives you more power than the Solo or Electron card which you might have had before.

You will certainly want something called a 'current' account. This is one where you can get your money out instantly. You may also want a 'deposit' or 'savings' account. This is one where you may not be able to get money out instantly, but it will pay you interest, a percentage of the money you have in the account.

> **NOTE:** Many building societies now offer the same facilities as banks, so take a look at the **Building society accounts** section ➡ page 24 before leaping into a bank.

How to choose a bank

There's not a huge difference between all the main banks. One thing's for sure: they all want you to sign up with them. If you think you haven't got nearly enough money to be important to them, think again. It used to be said that during your lifetime you would be more likely to get divorced than change your bank. Nowadays, people do change their banks a bit more often, but the banks still try very hard to grab you as a young customer – so that when you are rich and successful you will stay with them. The banks want your money. Never forget that.

Everyone else wants your money too. That's why you have to know how to look after it.

Anyway, go into a couple of banks. Tell them you want to open an account. If you are a student or on a gap year, tell them this – they usually have special facilities and perks for students, because they hope you will be a high-earner later on. Presumably, you hope this too. They will give you lots of leaflets. Go away and read them. These are the things to look out for:

➤ Does this bank have a branch near where you will be? Not essential, because you can take money out from cash machines in lots of different places. But it can be useful, especially if you don't have access to the Internet or a phone.

➤ Can you get cash out of a cash machine that is not that bank's machine? Most of the main banks share cash machines, but if you choose a more unusual bank, you may find you have to *pay* to get money out of a different bank's machine – definitely a bad idea. Each cash machine will have pictures of the cards and banks which can use that machine free. Check out the cash machines near where you live and/or work.

➤ What happens if you become 'overdrawn'? That's when you take more money out than you actually have, perhaps by writing a cheque when you thought you had enough money, or if a direct debit goes through and you didn't get round to paying in your birthday present from Aunty Jane. The bank may offer a free overdraft facility, which means that you will not have to pay bank charges (➡ page 21) if you go overdrawn, as long as you do not go overdrawn by more than the amount agreed. Some banks will let you go accidentally overdrawn by a certain amount without charging you – this is very useful because anyone can make a mistake. But others will charge you the minute you go a penny over.

➤ Will they offer you a loan, if necessary? How easy will this be? What will the interest rate be for that? What about a student loan? Gap year loan? Graduate loan?

➤ What is the rate of interest on the deposit or savings account? You need to ask what the APR is (➡ page 25). Note: rates of interest change. They can go up or down. There is very little difference, however, between the rates that the main banks offer. When one goes up, the others usually do as well.

➤ Does the current account also pay you interest? Some do, though the rate is usually tiny, so if you have *spare* money it should go in a deposit or savings account.

➤ Apart from an unauthorized overdraft, what else might incur bank charges? (➡ page 21.)

➤ What sort of card will you get? Maestro/Delta? A credit card?

➤ Do they have a telephone banking service with a free (usually 0800) or local rate (usually 0845) phoneline? This is extremely useful – you can transfer money between accounts, pay a bill, ask how much money you have, and ask any questions at all, usually 24 hours a day.

This all sounds quite complicated. But, as I said, there is very little difference between what the main banks offer. You will notice, especially if you are a student, that each bank may offer you a reward if you join them. If you can't find any other difference, why not accept the one that offers the gift you most want? But *never* let this over-ride any other reason. A bottle of champagne is soon consumed and a £10 M&S voucher soon spent.

To compare banks and what they offer, visit the website Support4Learning at www.support4learning.org.uk/money/banks.htm.

Internet banking?

An Internet-based bank may offer better interest rates because it does not have the cost of branches. But one downside is that sometimes you can't get on-line. Check how easy it will be to get money out, based on where you live, your own lifestyle, access to a reliable computer and the cost when you use the Internet. A personal recommendation would be good too – if it worked for your friend, it could well work for you.

However, you also have to consider the safety of your money. With the continual battle between the banks and the fraudsters, there's the risk of something going wrong with on-line banking – though this applies to 'normal' banks, too. You shouldn't have to worry too much, as any loss which is not your fault will be refunded to you, but it is something to consider and I would certainly only use an established company with lots of happy customers.

In short, if you have free and easy access to the Internet and use of a reliable computer, as well as easy access to a cash machine which the particular Internet bank is affiliated to, Internet banking is a good value option. Otherwise, stick to a high street bank.

> **!** **WARNING:** Be very careful about whether this is a legitimate bank. If you receive an unsolicited or spam advert or message, do not reply and *never* give any information about yourself on-line or by phone, unless you are 100% sure that this is legitimate.

YOUR MONEY

Ethical banking?

You might want to choose a bank with 'ethical policies', for example, one which avoids investing its money (your money) in companies perceived to be unethical, such as tobacco companies; or one which makes a point of investing in fair-trade ventures. You may hear this called 'green banking' or 'socially responsible investment' (SRI). If you want to use such a bank, that's great, but there are two downsides: sometimes this is simply an advertising ploy and if you look very closely you may find that the bank's view of what's ethical may differ from your view; and secondly, if you are saving money in such a bank, the rate of interest you receive (➡ page 25) *may* be less good than other banks.

> **!** **WARNING TO ALL BANK ACCOUNT HOLDERS:** If anyone phones, emails or texts you and asks for your bank account or credit card number, *never* give it. If they say they are phoning from your bank or credit card company, they are *not* – because if they were, they would know your account number and credit card number. They would also know your address, so do not give this either. Obviously, if *you* phone your bank or credit card company you *will* need to give such information so that they know who you are.

Bank charges

The good news is rather surprising: banking is free, as long as you have money in your account. You pay nothing for the chequebooks, statements, advice, cheque guarantee card or debit card. (There may be an annual fee for the credit card: ➡ page 31.) However, if you go overdrawn, by even £1 over your agreed overdraft limit (if you have one), you will then pay bank charges. These can mount up because quite often you then pay for *each* transaction – for example, each time you take money out.

As I mentioned above, some banks will allow you to go slightly overdrawn without charging you. This is definitely worth checking out before you sign up.

✱ TIP: If you are having temporary problems, speak to your bank before this becomes obvious. They will be much more sympathetic and helpful if you are honest.

❗ WARNING: If you pay money in and take money out on the same day, the money will come *out* of your account before the other money goes *in*. This means that if you think you are paying some money in to cover an outgoing amount, you may be overdrawn briefly and incur charges. Pay money in several days (usually 3–4) before you need it.

Your bank statement

You will receive a bank statement, usually each month. This will list every transaction you have made, including direct debits and any charges. You should check every item carefully – mistakes *can* happen and it is up to you to notice them. Keep all your Maestro/Delta receipts and receipts from cash machine withdrawals and always fill in the counterfoil (the bit that stays in the chequebook when you tear a cheque out) or the section at the front of your chequebook, whichever you have, when you write a cheque.

Writing a cheque

Points to remember:

➤ If you make a mistake, alter it and sign or initial the change.

➤ Make sure you have written the amount very clearly and that there is no room for someone to add something (like a zero…).

➤ Always write in the name of the payee and the amount before you sign it – if you sign a cheque with no amount in it, it is a 'blank cheque' and if it gets into the wrong hands, someone could simply fill in their own name and any amount they fancy.

➤ A 'crossed cheque' is one with two lines going through the words, and with '&co' written between the lines. It means that it cannot be exchanged for cash by someone who finds it. This is a useful safeguard because if you lose a cheque it is fairly useless to anyone who finds it. All cheques nowadays are printed like this so you don't have to worry about it – I just mention it because sometimes you are asked to send a crossed cheque. Just make sure it has these two lines on it – it will.

➤ When writing the amount in words, it's normal to put the number of pence as a number, not word. For example, 'one hundred and twenty-one pounds and 08p'.

➤ When writing an exact number of pounds, most people write 'only' after it. This is to stop someone adding a number of pence. For example, 'ten pounds only'.

➤ It's a good idea to fill all the rest of the writing space up with a line, so that no one can add anything. For example, '———Ten pounds and 70p———'

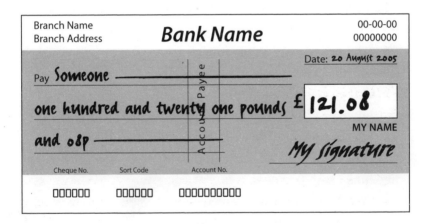

Building society accounts

A building society used to be a place where you could either borrow or save money. Some building societies are still exactly that. But many also have the same services as banks (usually because they have merged with a high street bank). In fact, there's often very little difference between what a bank can offer you and what a building society can offer – choose whichever seems more convenient for you.

You can compare them in exactly the same way as you compare banks: go in and ask for some leaflets. Tell them:

➤ whether you are a student;
➤ whether you earn;
➤ whether you are looking for ordinary banking services or whether you already have a bank account somewhere else and just want to save in the building society.

The main differences between the different savings accounts will be:

➤ how much warning you have to give when you want to take money out;
➤ how much interest they pay.

You will get a higher rate of interest for an account where you have to give longer warning.

IMPORTANT POINT: Normally, the interest you earn on all accounts at bank or building societies is taxed. The tax is taken off before you get the interest. But if you are not a tax-payer because your earnings are too low, you have to register to receive your interest without the tax taken off. Ask the bank or building society for a form.

Interest

Banks and building societies use your money while you leave it with them. They use it to make money for themselves, which is how they manage to provide you with a free banking service. If you leave your money in a deposit or savings account, they will pay you interest – a percentage of what you leave there. If they say that interest is 'calculated daily', that doesn't mean they pay you 0.01p each day and send it round to you in a security van with an armed guard. It means that each day the computer works out what you've got, and keeps the interest for you until either a) the date comes round when they pay interest or b) you close your account. So you do not lose money by closing your account in one month rather than another (unless it is something called a 'fixed-term account' – this is an account where you agree to leave the money untouched for a certain period).

You also need to understand about interest when you are thinking about credit cards or loans – because *you* will then be paying interest to the bank or whoever gave you the loan. And one thing is certain, the rate of interest *you* will pay is rather a lot more than the amount they will pay you when you let them use your money. It's just the way it works. And quite fair when you consider they've got to pay all the people who look after your money and smile at you so pleasantly when you bring them more.

More about this in the section on **Credit cards:** ➡ page 29.

APR

APR stands for Annual Percentage Rate. When you compare the financial services of any company, whether it's to give them your money or to borrow money from them (as in a credit card), it's the APR that you need to compare. When you are giving them your money, you want as high an APR as possible; with credit cards and loans you want a low one.

Gross or net?

Gross is the bizarre word that means 'complete', or 'without the tax – or other deduction – taken off'. Net is the less bizarre but equally unhelpful word which means 'the figure once all charges or deductions are made'. It is sometimes spelt nett. Building society and bank savings interest is usually paid net. (But ➡ **National Savings account** page 27.)

If interest is paid to you net but you are a non-taxpayer, ask the bank or building society for a form so that you can have the interest paid gross, thereby not paying tax when you don't have to.

If you work irregular hours and can't predict whether you will be earning enough to pay tax, you should have interest paid net, and then claim the tax back by filling in a tax return (ask at your local Inland Revenue Enquiry Centre).

Saving

If you can possibly save, do it. You can save for whatever you want: a holiday, a new stereo or a rainy day. No, not actually rainy days – just days when there's not much money around and you need your savings.

Don't save your money in a jar. Well, you could, but it could be stolen. Even more likely, you could spend it on something very boring.

Save in a savings or deposit account at your bank or building society. You will earn interest and because you can't just pop in and take it out, it will tend to stay there. And grow. And grow. If you are not a taxpayer, remember to ask to register to have your interest paid 'gross'.

National Savings account

Another good place to save, especially if you are a non-tax-payer, is in a National Savings account. You do this through a post office. The reason it is good for non-taxpayers is that the interest is paid to you without the tax being deducted, i.e. gross.

If you are in a very lucky position and can save quite seriously, consider taking out something like a mini cash ISA (Individual Savings Account). Since most people just leaving home are not in this position, I'm not going to go into the details – phew! – but you'll get information from your own bank or building society. The best thing about ISAs is that you do not pay tax on the gains they make.

Debit cards

A debit card is one where the money comes directly from your account when you pay for something. You do not receive a bill because you are in effect paying for it instantly, almost like paying cash. Maestro and Delta are the most common. If you had a Solo or Electron card before, you use Maestro and Delta in the same way – though they are accepted in very many more places; almost everywhere, in fact.

The differences between Solo or Electron and Maestro or Delta are that with Maestro or Delta you can:

➤ take more cash out in one day – ask how much;
➤ buy as many things as you want during any one day, as long as you have the money in your account (or an overdraft facility);
➤ use it in more shops, as well as restaurants and for buying things by phone or on-line;
➤ use it as a cheque guarantee card (when you pay for something by cheque in a shop, you will be asked for your card).

Credit cards (and store cards)

There are two main types of credit card:

➤ Those issued by a bank or a finance company – the most common cards of this sort are Mastercard and Visa. Some of the major supermarkets now offer Mastercard or Visa too through their own finance companies – these are not the same as 'store cards'. Mastercard and Visa can be used in shops, restaurants, garages and other outlets all over the world, and you can buy things by phone or on the Internet.

➤ Those issued by a shop or store, usually called store cards. These credit cards can only be used in that store, or a store within the same group of companies.

When used properly, credit cards of the first type are an excellent way to manage your expenses. When you buy something on a credit card, you do not pay for it immediately. Depending on when your credit card company sends its bill, you could have up to 59 days before you actually pay. Then, if you pay the *full amount* before the deadline, you pay no interest at all.

However, and it really is the most enormous *however* you have ever heard, *if you do not pay the full amount* you will then pay interest on the rest. And the interest rate can be quite high. This is the reason why many people get into serious trouble with credit card debt. It is so horribly easy for your debt to mount up. You buy something else, don't pay that off, and the interest just grows and grows.

The worst thing is to have several credit cards. If you tend to be a spender more than a saver, don't take out a credit card at all. If you have one, cut it up. Now. And if your credit card bill is already starting to drag you down, ➡ the section on **Debt problems,** page 54.

What about store cards?

Watch out – the APR is usually higher (though one or two offer very good rates). You've probably had the experience of going to buy some clothes and being asked if you want to save 10% by taking out their free credit card. Fine, do it, enjoy your 10% discount – then, as soon as you leave the shop, cut the card into tiny pieces and get ready to pay the bill off in full when it arrives.

Are there any other advantages to credit cards?

Yes, there are actually.

➤ It's safer than carrying cash. If you lose your credit card, and someone finds it and uses it, you simply telephone the special number straight away. After that, you will only lose the first £50 that is stolen (and maybe nothing at all).

➤ If an item is over £100 and you have a problem with it (➡ pages 271–2), the credit card company has to help you even if the shop/supplier will not. The credit card company will arrange your refund (if you are entitled to it ➡ **Customers and the law** pages 271–2). This is not the case with a debit card.

➤ Some credit cards give you points depending on how much you spend. The points may then mount up into vouchers. This can seem like good value, but remember that they are only doing it because they have worked out that you will spend more that way. Unless you can be incredibly disciplined and only ever buy what you need, don't be taken in by points and rewards.

➤ Similarly, some cards give you air miles depending on how much you spend. These can then be exchanged for free air tickets. Again, don't be tempted to spend more

YOUR MONEY

just because you are dreaming of sipping cocktails on a Caribbean beach.

➤ There may be other benefits, such as free travel insurance, if you book a holiday using your credit card – but take a look at the small print: you may have to book the *whole* holiday on your card; and the benefits may be less attractive than with other travel insurance. ➥ **Travel insurance** page 48.

Affinity cards

Affinity cards are credit cards and work in exactly the same way. The only difference is that the company pays a small amount to a particular charity for you. A nice idea, but check the interest rates, as they can be higher. Also, this 'small amount' is usually pitifully small. To be honest, you might be better going with a different card and actually donating some money to a charity yourself.

Credit cashback cards

Some credit cards actually pay a small amount of what you spend back to you – a very small percentage, of course. A very nice idea but, again, watch out for the interest rates if you don't pay the full amount each month.

Other things to know about credit cards

➤ Some credit card companies charge you an annual fee. Though this is not large (usually about £10), why choose an account like this if you don't have to? Shop around.

➤ On your bill, it will show a 'minimum payment'. You *must* pay this on time – the easiest way is to set up a direct debit (➥ page 36) to pay the minimum off automatically. If you don't pay in time, you may incur an extra charge, which can be quite significant (for example, £25), as well as being charged extra interest. If you still fail to pay, your card will be stopped. This will also affect your credit rating – ➡ page 39 – and you will have trouble getting another credit card, loan or mortgage.

➤ Your credit card will allow you to withdraw cash from a cash machine. BEWARE: you will be charged interest immediately, even if you pay the amount in full when the bill arrives. And the interest rate will usually be *higher* than the normal rate.

➤ Interest rates can change. Up or down.

➤ Some credit cards will offer a low APR for the first few months, but it then rises. Check the small print. And ➡ the **0% credit?** section below.

0% credit?

Question: I've heard about 0% credit cards. That sounds amazing. Is it?

Answer: Possibly, with conditions. Some credit cards offer you 0% interest for the first six months. Obviously, that's great. For six months. But there are two possible problems:

➤ You might well be tempted to spend *more* in those six months.

➤ After the six months, the rate will probably be *higher* than normal.

So, a 0% card is certainly a great idea *if – and only if – you are sure you will pay off the whole debt during that time.*

Question: What about this clever idea? Why don't I take out a 0% card, then after five months switch it all to a different 0% card? Then I spend, spend, spend and – hey presto – five months later, I switch again. Over the next five years I have huge fun racking up a seriously enormous debt, but never pay a penny of interest to any of the credit card companies stupid enough to fall for my trick.

Answer: First, you don't want a seriously enormous debt, believe me. If you don't get on top of debt, it buries you. Second, you will find it impossible to follow this plan because your credit rating will be wrecked after the first or second move. No credit company will want to take you on if they see your pattern, because they'll know they are not going to get any money out of you, which is what they want more than anything. Otherwise, why on earth do you think they exist? To keep you in champagne and beach holidays? Er, no. For how to deal with debt problems ➡ page 54.

In short: Credit cards are only ideal if you have enough money to pay off the full amount each month. Small items mount up and it can be difficult to remember what you owe, and easy to keep on spending. If you need to borrow money, it will probably work out much cheaper to take out a loan from your own bank.

Card protection and fraud

There are several ways that criminals can take money using your card. They could actually steal your card, or they could steal the details of your card and use it without you even knowing – and your card will still be safe in your wallet. You have some strategies to help you.

If you find that your card is missing, phone the number given *straight away*. If you can't find the number, phone the bank or company that issued your card. You can use the phone-banking number, if you know it, or you can look in the phone book for the bank's number. From the moment you phone, you are not responsible for any losses, apart from the first £50, at the most.

What if you don't notice that your card is missing immediately? Don't panic. If your card company notices an unusual pattern of spending, they will contact you. If you don't realize you've lost your card, but the bill arrives and you suddenly realize there are a huge number of things on it which you didn't buy, contact your company immediately. You may be pleasantly surprised to know that you *probably* will not be liable for these. The fraud part of the company will investigate, and unless you have been particularly careless, they will usually only ask you for £50. However, this is something you should ask when you take out the card, as it is possible that some companies might not be so understanding.

If your details have been stolen electronically and you still have your card, you will certainly not have to pay for peculiar items that appear on your bill. Simply phone the card company when you get your bill.

Consider taking out card protection. (You will be offered this when you take out a credit card – one fee covers *all* your cards, however, so don't pay this more than once.) For a small annual fee, you will be given one phone number to phone if you lose any card – and you will then be liable for no further losses. This is really only an advantage if you have several cards. It covers other cards, too, such as your Maestro/Delta card, and even things like your passport.

How to minimize the risk of fraud

➤ Don't let your card out of your sight. This means that, in a shop or restaurant, you should be able to watch them swipe your card. Say you do not want it to leave your sight – tell them you've been a victim of fraud and you've been told to do it this way. Of course, most restaurants and shops do not have criminals working in them. But some do. And they will not have 'I am a shady criminal' written on their foreheads.

➤ Keep your card in a place where you will see it often, so you will notice if it has gone. In your purse/wallet is the obvious place, not loose in a pocket or a drawer.

➤ When you get your card, write the emergency phone number in several places, not just in your purse (your purse might be stolen…).

➤ If someone phones you and says they are from your credit card company and they think your card might be used fraudulently, be careful: if they ask for your credit card number, don't give it to them. If it was really your credit card company, they'd know it! Contact the company immediately and report it.

➤ On the Internet, only use companies you trust.

➤ As mentioned in the warning on page 20, never give your bank details out to someone who contacts you.

YOUR MONEY

Direct debits and standing orders

Direct debits and standing orders are very good ways to pay regular bills. Once you set one up, the bill is paid automatically, so you don't have to think about it or make a phone call or write a cheque. They can also be a good way to spread a large annual bill into monthly or quarterly payments, so you can plan and budget better.

However, you do need to have money in your account, otherwise a standing order would be missed or, worse, a direct debit would incur a bank charge. So, if your finances are dodgy, you should probably avoid direct debits.

The difference between direct debits and standing orders

A direct debit is set up by the supplier of the goods or services, with you signing the form. It usually allows the supplier to change the amount – so, for example, if you pay your gas bill by direct debit, it will be a different amount each month, depending on how much gas you used. (However, it is often possible to set up a direct debit for a fixed amount per month, so that you can budget – ask the company concerned.)

A standing order is set up by you, the payer. It is useful if you want to pay a fixed amount each month (or whenever), for example to save money by transferring it into a savings account. You simply tell your bank that you want to transfer a set amount each month/quarter/year into a particular account (whether yours or someone else's).

You can cancel a direct debit or standing order at any time. Contact your bank, by phone or in person.

> **NOTE:** If a direct debit goes through your account when you do not have enough money in the account, you will go overdrawn and incur bank charges. A standing order simply will not go through if there is no money there.

As long as your finances are healthy (i.e. you do not tend to have a virtually empty or overdrawn bank account and as long as you are not paying bank charges for each transaction), I recommend that you set up direct debits for all your regular bills: phone, mobile, gas, electricity, water, council tax and insurance. You can even pay your rent like this. If you do this, it makes life easier and allows you to spread your costs and budget better.

> **NOTE:** With direct debits for bills which are different each month, such as gas, electricity and credit cards, you will be sent a bill a few days before the direct debit goes through, so you can see how much it is. For direct debit payments that are the same each month (or each quarter or year, depending on how often you pay), you will not receive a bill, so it is up to you to make a note to remind yourself that this payment will go through. Watch out for any that are paid annually – they may take you by surprise if you don't make a note to remind yourself.

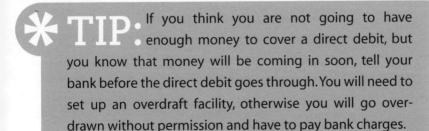

TIP: If you think you are not going to have enough money to cover a direct debit, but you know that money will be coming in soon, tell your bank before the direct debit goes through. You will need to set up an overdraft facility, otherwise you will go overdrawn without permission and have to pay bank charges.

Paying bills

I've mentioned the idea of paying bills by direct debit. What else is there to say about paying bills? It's not exactly complicated or amazing.

> ➤ Pay them – by the deadline.
> ➤ If you can't pay, contact the company concerned. They can withdraw their services (though they would warn you and give you some opportunities to pay – your water won't be cut off when you are two days overdue).
> ➤ Know what payments are going to be coming up. Look ahead. Ask for help if you can't manage.

Credit rating

Everyone has a credit rating. Most people don't know what theirs is. A credit rating is a system of points which companies use to decide whether you are someone they want to lend their money to. When you apply for credit or a loan, or when you start a building society account, and in some other circumstances too, the company concerned will check your rating, using a credit rating agency. If it's not good enough, they may not give you what you are asking for. It is their decision.

Things that will affect your credit rating include:

➤ your salary;
➤ your employment history;
➤ whether you have credit from several sources;
➤ whether you have failed to make any minimum payments (they are quite happy for you not to make *full* payments, because that's how they make money – on the interest you pay);
➤ whether you have any court orders against you. These are usually called County Court Judgements or CCJs and happen if you are taken to court for non-payment of a bill or rent;
➤ the credit rating of someone you are 'associated' with (➡ **Association** page 40).

Checking or changing your credit rating

If someone refuses to give you credit or any financial services, ask whether a credit rating agency was used – and which one, because different agencies use slightly different methods. You have a legal right to this information and you must be told how to contact the agency. You then *should* contact the agency – because there might be a mistake on your credit history or rating, which you are then allowed to change. You may have to pay a small fee (approx £2), but it's worth it.

Association: your credit rating may be affected if you are regarded as 'associated' with someone who has a bad credit rating. This could be someone living at the same address or someone related to you; or it could simply be that the street, block or area you live in is regarded as a bad risk. If you discover that this is the case, and if you can show that your finances are nothing to do with the other person/people, you can apply to become 'disassociated'. This simply means that your credit history is now separate from theirs.

How to disassociate: if you have been refused credit, find out which credit rating agency was used (see above) and tell them you want to write a 'letter of disassociation'. If you have not yet been refused credit but suspect you may be associated wrongly with someone with poor credit, contact one of the agencies below and check.

Try:
➤ **Experian**, P.O. Box 8000, Nottingham, NG1 5GX
➤ **Equifax**, Department IE, P.O. Box 3001, Glasgow, G81 2DT
➤ www.fiscuscreditcards.co.uk
➤ www.CheckMyFile.com
They all provide excellent advice.

If the information on your credit record is wrong in any way, you can arrange for it to be changed – so you will have to show that it is wrong. And if it is correct but unattractive, see if there's anything you can do to improve it (such as paying money that you owe). It will take a month for changes to go through.

Having a bad credit rating is a real nuisance. But you can improve it and eventually make it beautiful and healthy by following the guidelines below.

- ➤ Never fail to make minimum payments on credit cards.
- ➤ Don't pay late.
- ➤ Don't chop and change between companies.
- ➤ Don't take out too many credit cards/loans.
- ➤ Keep your finances as well-controlled as possible.
- ➤ Try to earn more, and always declare your earnings for tax and NI (➡ page 42).
- ➤ Apply to have a CCJ (➡ page 39) removed once it has expired – ask at a Citizen's Advice Bureau.

But remember, no one has the right to credit – it is entirely up to the lender to decide. It is up to you to show that you are a reliable person who will always pay back their money. It's like borrowing from friends – if you have a reputation for not paying money back, no one is going to want to lend you any.

1

YOUR MONEY

Tax and National Insurance

Everyone who earns more than a certain amount a year must pay income tax and National Insurance (NI). If you are an employee, this will be sorted for you by your employer. Tax is deducted from your pay – this is called PAYE, or Pay as You Earn. If you do not receive a proper wage slip detailing your pay and the tax and NI deducted, your employer is breaking the law. This is called 'cash in hand' and is a way for your employer and you to avoid paying the correct taxes. It is illegal and if you are discovered, your employer faces prosecution. If you knew, or should have suspected that this was going on, you face prosecution.

The 'certain amount' I referred to in the previous paragraph varies. The Inland Revenue (the organization that works out the amount of tax each person must pay) tells you what this amount is in something called your tax code. Everyone is entitled to earn some money before paying any tax. For example, everyone has something called the 'personal allowance' (£4895 for the 2005/6 tax year). This means that if you don't earn more than this in a year, you will not pay any income tax. If you do pay some tax, and then lose your job and find that you have earned less than the personal allowance, the excess tax you paid will be repaid to you – *though you will need to ask for it*, by filling in a tax return. (See below.)

For more details about income tax, PAYE, tax codes and NI, see the Inland Revenue website at www.inlandrevenue.gov.uk and the Citizens Advice Bureau website at www.adviceguide.org.uk. For individual information relevant to you, go to or phone your local Inland Revenue Enquiry Centre (details in **Troubleshoot** page 59).

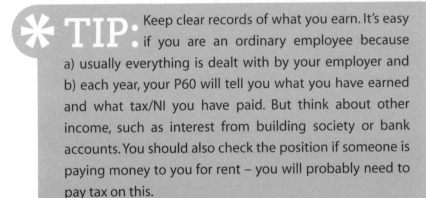

WARNING: It is your responsibility to make sure you are paying the right amount of tax. It is not the Inland Revenue's responsibility to find out unless you ask. And they have long memories and long arms – they can come looking for you years later. If in doubt, phone your local Inland Revenue Enquiry Centre, as above.

TIP: Keep clear records of what you earn. It's easy if you are an ordinary employee because a) usually everything is dealt with by your employer and b) each year, your P60 will tell you what you have earned and what tax/NI you have paid. But think about other income, such as interest from building society or bank accounts. You should also check the position if someone is paying money to you for rent – you will probably need to pay tax on this.

Evasion or avoidance?

You may think that evading something is the same as avoiding. Not in tax law. Avoiding means finding a *legal* way to pay less tax. For example, by saving in an ISA (➡ page 27), you avoid paying tax on the gains. This is perfectly legal. Evading means trying to escape paying tax through an illegal means. For example, not declaring everything you earn is evasion and therefore illegal. If you are caught, you face prosecution.

What is a tax return?

Employees who pay tax through PAYE and who do not earn any other money will not normally need to fill in a tax return. This is a form that some people (such as the self-employed) have to fill in once a year, declaring all their income so that the Inland Revenue can work out their tax. It is your responsibility to discover whether you should fill one out, so if you are in any doubt ask at your local Inland Revenue Enquiry Centre (contact details in the **Troubleshoot** section ➡ page 59). You will also need to fill one in if you have paid too much tax – this could happen if you lost your job and didn't find another one, or if you paid tax on the interest you earned on a savings account, when actually you were a non-taxpayer – ➡ the sections on **Building society accounts** and **Gross or net?** pages 24–6.

YOUR MONEY

1

Insurance

Everyone hates paying for insurance. But how much more would you hate to be burgled and lose everything? Or for a burst water pipe or fire to destroy your carpets, furniture, clothes, MP3 player, stereo and computer. You might think you don't own very much, but the average student burglary is worth £900.

What is insurance exactly? You pay an amount of money to a company to 'cover' a specific type of possession or disaster. If nothing happens, the company keeps your money. If the disaster happens, they pay you the agreed amount. As long as you have fulfilled everything in the insurance policy – read the small print. Very, very carefully.

What can I insure? You *can* insure virtually anything, but don't. The main types of insurance are:

➤ Buildings – if you are in rented accommodation, your landlord will deal with this and you pay your share through the rent. This covers damage to the actual building – including roof, windows, doors – and permanent fixtures, such as your sink or bath. This is essential insurance.

➤ Contents/possessions – this is the most important insurance for you to consider. It's not compulsory but can be very cheap since you probably don't own all that much. Very highly recommended – you'd be silly not to.

➤ Life/critical illness – completely unnecessary at your age, unless you have a child who would need financial support if you died.

➤ Car – you have to have third party insurance (to cover damage that you cause to someone else). Anything else is optional and whether you choose to take it out will depend on what you can afford and how important your car is to you.

➤ Travel – if you book a holiday, most travel companies will insist on travel insurance. If they don't, seriously consider buying it (but shop around). If they do insist, you do not have to take their insurance – but you will have to provide evidence that you have adequate cover.

What is a 'premium'? The premium is the amount you pay for the insurance.

What is an 'excess'? The excess is the amount that the company will not pay when you make a claim. So, if your 'excess' is £150, they will not pay the first £150 of any claim. (In other words, it would be pointless to claim anything below this.)

Contents/possessions insurance

Points to consider:

➤ Shop around. There are huge differences in cover and cost.

➤ Consider using an insurance broker. This is someone who can find insurance for you. You pay the broker a fee, but it *may* work out cheaper because a broker may be able to get a better deal. Ask what the broker can do for you and see if it is better than what you can do yourself.

➤ When estimating the value of your possessions, give the true figure. If you only insure part of the value, they will not pay the full value.

➤ Read the conditions very, very carefully. For example, it may say that you must have all windows closed at night apart from the bedroom. If so, and if a burglar enters through your open bathroom window, the insurance company will not have to pay a penny. Similarly with using a burglar alarm: if you have one but don't set it, the company may not pay out.

➤ Does the policy require you to change anything in your property before you are covered? For example, it might require you to have specific locks – what would this cost you?

➤ Does the policy offer 'new-for-old' replacement? If so, this means that if your five-year-old stereo is stolen, they pay for you to get a brand-new one. You must consider this when estimating the value of everything when you take out the policy – the value is then *what it would cost to replace*. 'New-for-old' cover is more expensive – but usually worth it, because otherwise the money you receive in the event of a fire or theft will not be enough for you to replace items.

➤ 'All-risks' is a very useful part of the policy. It covers the items you might naturally take out of the house, such as your camera, mobile phone, coat or jewellery. You may have to list these items and give their value (though usually only very valuable items). You may have to pay extra – if so, you can choose whether or not to opt for this part. If you have a bike, check this is covered. Bikes are often stolen.

➤ 'Accidental damage' is something you would pay extra for, but it's worth considering, if you can afford it. It means that if you somehow drop the television – unlikely but possible – it should be covered.

➤ Note whether you have any items that have to be listed separately, such as a computer or valuable musical instrument.

➤ If some items are used as part of your work or business, you may have to say this – it shouldn't affect the cost but there could be something in the small print about this.

➤ Read the small print. Then get out a magnifying glass and read it again. Lots of things will not be covered and there will be conditions.

You can often make your insurance cheaper by having proper window locks, living in a neighbourhood watch area and having a burglar alarm (but then you *have* to set it every time you go out).

Car insurance

Read the terms of your car insurance policy extra carefully and if there is anything you don't understand, ask (as with anything). One important thing about car insurance is the 'no-claims bonus'. The company will offer you a reduced premium if you do not make a claim. If you do make a claim, you lose this bonus for a certain amount of time (perhaps three years), meaning that your premium will be higher. This means that you should think very carefully about whether to claim if the damage is minor – it is often better not to, so as to avoid losing your no-claims bonus.

NOTE: ➡ pages 269 and 313 for what to do in the case of a car accident. You must report all incidents which involve another person's property, or injury to any person or animal, to the police.

Travel insurance

Shop around and read the small print. Cover should include:
➤ all medical costs in the event of accident and illness;
➤ loss/theft of possessions;
➤ cancellation of the holiday.

NOTE: If you are travelling to a European Union country, you need to get an E111 card. Apply for this from a post office. Take it with you on holiday. This entitles you to treatment in that country. *However*, it only allows the same free treatment that people of that country are entitled to. So if a country does not provide free medicines to its citizens, you will have to pay for these too. So, you should still have insurance.

Extended warranties

This is when you buy a large item, such as a television, and the shop offers to extend the guarantee for an extra two years (for example). One word springs to mind and that is 'bargepole'. As in, 'don't touch it with one'. They are, almost always, poor value. I might even call some of them a rip-off.

Why? First, because the first year after buying a new electrical item is nearly always free anyway. So, when they talk about a three-year guarantee, they really mean two extra years. Second, it works out extremely expensive. Third, the risk measurement almost never makes sense.

Let me explain (and it would be nice if the extremely aggressive man in a major electrical store I was in recently would read this and inwardly digest it): a typical home owner or tenant might have the following major items: TV, video/DVD player, stereo, oven, hob, microwave, washing machine, vacuum cleaner, computer, printer, fridge and freezer. That's twelve items. (And you might have more, such as an MP3 player or dishwasher.) I estimated what extended warranties would have cost on these twelve items. The total came to around £1400. I have all these items. I took out an extended warranty on none of them. None of them went wrong during the second two years. I saved £1400.

If something had gone wrong with a couple of them, it is inconceivable that repairs would have cost me £1400. And that's just in two years. By the time you are middle-aged, you'll have had several new versions of all of these items and hardly any of them will have gone wrong within the first three years – it's usually the *next* three years when they start going wrong, and you wouldn't be covered for that. In fact, when I start to work out what I've saved, I feel a warm glow come over me.

Time to go and reward myself. I did see a rather nice laptop the other day... Must remember to say no to the extended warranty.

Of course, you could be unlucky. It is the fear of extraordinary bad luck that the extended warranty people want to encourage. You would be far better putting the money you would have paid for the warranties into a savings account and watching it grow – use it if you do need to repair or replace something, and if you don't, enjoy it.

Mobile phones are a slightly different case. The situation and approaches of the various mobile phone companies keep changing, but at the time of writing, the situation is as follows. The first 3–6 months are free. After one year, you *usually* do not need further cover because you can get a new phone anyway, for nothing if you choose one which is on a free offer at that time. So if you take out their extended warranty (which they call insurance, because basically that's what all extended warranties are), you really only need it for 6–9 months. When you consider that your household contents insurance *may well* cover the loss or theft of your phone while you're out of the house (under the 'All-risks' bit – ➡ page 47), then you are paying only for the chance of *damage or failure* during those nine months. It's up to you whether you think it is worth paying for.

Very occasionally, you will come across an extended warranty that actually feels like good value. By this, I mean cheap and offering cover on a large item. This has happened to me. Once. It is also sometimes possible to negotiate a much lower cost on an extended warranty. This has also happened to me. Twice. Ask, and you may receive. And if they say no, you say no. They don't like that.

Budgeting

Budgeting simply means knowing what your expenses are and what your income is, and balancing the two so that there's always a bit more income than expense. If only actually doing it were so simple.

Here are the outgoings (expenses) you need to think about. Work out each one on a monthly basis. Then see if it comes to less than your monthly income. If it does, smile. If it doesn't…

➤ Rent/mortgage
➤ Council tax
➤ Water rates
➤ Gas
➤ Electricity
➤ Telephone
➤ Mobile phone
➤ Insurance
➤ Food
➤ Cleaning/household items
➤ Travel
➤ Car, if you have one – include the cost of possible repairs and annual servicing, insurance, road tax and petrol
➤ Personal – toiletries, hair appointments, etc.
➤ Entertainment
➤ Clothes and shoes
➤ Books and stationery
➤ Birthday presents and Christmas presents
➤ Replacing items – a good way to work this out is to add up the value of major things that might have to be replaced and work out 10%. That is called the 'depreciation' of your possessions and if you allow this amount a

year, it will help you budget for replacements

➤ A herbal stress remedy for when you've added it all up.

Cutting expenses

Obviously, the first thing to do if the outgoings come to more than your income is to try to cut costs. There will be lots of things you buy that you don't actually need. One tip is to carry cash when you go shopping, and only take with you the amount you can afford to spend. Then you can't be tempted by an impulse purchase.

Well, that's too obvious. What about some other ways to cut your outgoings?

➤ Are you on the best tariff for phone and mobile phone? Ask the companies if they can offer a better tariff for you – or consider changing to a different company. (With a mobile phone, you'll need to make sure you've fulfilled your original contract first.) Say you are thinking of switching to another company unless they can come up with a more economical tariff for you. (The UK Power website – below – also provides this checking facility.)

➤ Are you with the cheapest gas and electricity providers? On the Internet, visit www.ukpower.co.uk or phone 0800 093 2447. You will be able to check, free.

➤ Do you know how much electricity or gas you are using each time you switch something on? ➡ **Cutting electricity bills** and **Cutting gas bills,** pages 53 and 54.

➤ If you are a student, are you making full use of student discounts? Ask your students' union or visit the NUS website at www.nusonline.co.uk for information about local offers.

➤ Simply don't buy brand names or designer labels. If you do, nine times out of ten you are being a victim of their marketing techniques. And at the very least, you are shelling out money that you could keep for yourself, and all for the sake of image. Stand firm. Resist. You are stronger than the ad-people.

➤ Don't respond to text messages or promotions that ask you to text or phone a number.

➤ 'Look after the pennies and the pounds will look after themselves.' It's an old and very irritating rule, but very true. It's the small savings you make that add up – and the small extras you buy that add up to a larger bill than you imagined. You don't have to make big savings in one go in order to make big savings in the end.

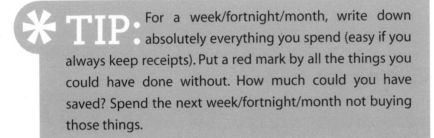

TIP: For a week/fortnight/month, write down absolutely everything you spend (easy if you always keep receipts). Put a red mark by all the things you could have done without. How much could you have saved? Spend the next week/fortnight/month not buying those things.

Cutting electricity bills

Although kettles and vacuum cleaners are amongst the most power-greedy items, you don't have them switched on very often, so they aren't the worst offenders. It's things like electric heaters, as well as dishwashers and washing machines that are the worst. There's an easy way to tell: look at the amount of 'watts' an item uses. Your electric heater might, for example, be a 2kW heater. This means it uses 2000 watts (2 kilowatts). A 100W light bulb obviously uses 100W. So, having your heater on for an hour is the same as having 20 bright lights on. Or 50 bedside lamps (they usually run on 40W bulbs). Having your heater on half-heat will use half that. It's still colossal. To work out how much it will cost you, 1kW uses a unit of electricity in one hour. You can find the cost of one unit on your electricity bill. Mine is currently 7.3p. So, a 2kW heater will cost me 14.6p an hour to run. Doesn't seem a lot, but it mounts up.

Ways to save electricity

➤ Switch things off when you don't need them.

➤ Use low-energy light bulbs (they cost more to buy but last *much* longer and cost less to run.

➤ Have your house well-insulated, so heat does not disappear through cracks and thin windows: thick curtains, draught-excluders, proper insulation – all these help.

You can also make a difference by doing things like only putting the minimum water necessary in the kettle, keeping electric rings as low as possible, using 40W bulbs where you don't need bright lights.

Cutting gas bills

It's not so easy to measure how much gas you use. However, you could experiment by reading your meter before you put the heating on; have it on for a few hours without doing anything else like cooking; then read your meter again. Your gas bill will tell you the cost of one unit. In this way, you can see what it costs you to have the heating on for a certain amount of time. However, there's no point doing this test in warm weather, as your thermostat will mean that the boiler is having to do less work.

Ways to save gas

➤ Turn the thermostat down a bit, so that the house does not reach such a great heat.

➤ Use good insulation, as for electricity.

➤ Keep gas rings on as low as possible.

➤ Set timer to come on a little later and go off a little earlier.

Debt problems

Sometimes, however hard you try, your money problems just won't go away. Debt is something which can just get worse and worse. It can also lead to real stress and depression. It can ruin lives and relationships.

It doesn't have to be like that. The first rule is: don't wait to get help. Visit your local Citizens Advice Bureau (CAB) or contact the National Debtline (contact details in **Troubleshoot** section ➡ page 59) before things feel too bad. They will help you work out the best way to get out of debt. And there are very definitely bad ways and good ways to deal with debt.

Some dos and don'ts:

➤ Don't ask for help from a financial company – though *do* tell your own bank/credit card company that you have a problem. Don't ask them to sort it out for you – ask the CAB – but it does help if they know. A debt management company can seem like a good idea at the time, but you will often pay a hefty fee. With the CAB you get free, completely independent advice.

➤ Do pay the important debts off first: those are the ones where the penalty for not paying will be worst, such as not paying rent or mortgage.

➤ Do investigate switching your credit card to one with low or 0% interest (but ➡ page 32).

➤ Don't try to work all this out on your own. Get help.

➤ Don't be embarrassed. If you have very little money coming in, how can you be expected to cope with debt?

➤ Don't try to gamble your way out of debt. Gambling includes the lottery and gaming cards – why do you think so many millions of pounds go to the good causes that the lottery helps? Because so many millions of people buy tickets each week and don't win.

The main problem with debt is the increasing interest you pay on it – so that even if you can afford to eat, live, pay the rent, etc., you can't afford the interest on your debt. And it grows. And grows. It doesn't go away without help.

Scams

This is quite simple really: if it seems too good to be true, it probably is. If anyone phones or writes to you to tell you you've won a guaranteed prize, you almost certainly haven't, however certain the caller sounds.

This is the sort of thing that can happen: you are told you've won a fantastic sports car. It's there in the picture. You can see it, gleaming and sleek and shiny. All you have to do is go and collect it at a swanky London hotel. When you get there, all excited, dreaming of speeding through the evening sunshine with the wind in your hair, you discover that after listening to five hours of droning sales talk about a timeshare in a country racked with civil war, you are indeed going to receive a fantastic sports car: literally a fantasy. The car you saw in the picture was a model, as in 'toy'. A palm-sized toy car. This has actually happened.

These things sound tempting. They are supposed to be. Just say no.

Signs that should make you suspicious

➤ Being told you only have a certain amount of time to claim your 'prize'.
➤ Being asked to phone a premium rate number – they usually start with 090.
➤ Being asked to send an 'administration' fee.
➤ The prize being offered in foreign currency.
➤ Being offered a prize for something you know you have not entered.

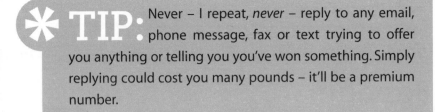

TIP: Never – I repeat, *never* – reply to any email, phone message, fax or text trying to offer you anything or telling you you've won something. Simply replying could cost you many pounds – it'll be a premium number.

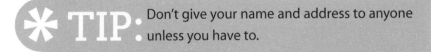

TIP: Don't give your name and address to anyone unless you have to.

TIP: To stop phone calls from companies trying to sell you a dream, or wanting to 'conduct a survey' (i.e. to get your details) sign up (free) to the Telephone Preference Service: www.tpsonline.org.uk or phone 0845 070 0707.

TIP: It is illegal to send unsolicited text messages – if you get one, do not follow its instructions. Do not text back. Do not phone the number given – this is often a premium line, which is incredibly expensive and is often set up to keep you on the line for minutes on end.

Benefits

We live in a country with a welfare state. It's designed to help anyone who needs help. If that's you, make sure you claim what you are entitled to. People in benefits offices don't go knocking on doors asking who *wants* some extra money – you have to go and claim it.

To find out whether you might be eligible for any benefits, visit the CAB or their excellent website at www.adviceguide.org.uk. They will explain all the different possibilities, such as Job-Seeker's Allowance, Income Support and Housing Benefit, any of which you could well be able to claim.

If you have a disability or a mobility problem, you are very likely to be eligible for special help. Ask. It's that simple.

Summary

Five simple rules cover all aspects of money and money problems.

> ➤ Ask advice from an independent organization such as the CAB.
> ➤ Shop around for the best buy.
> ➤ If it seems too good to be true, it probably is.
> ➤ Keep on top of things and be organized – half an hour a month of boring admin. could save you financial headache later.
> ➤ Read the small print. And then read it again.

Troubleshoot

Benefits Enquiry line

For any enquiry about benefits you may be eligible for.
Phone: 0800 882200
(N. Ireland – 0800 220674)

Citizens Advice Bureau

UK-wide organization
providing free and professional
advice on a huge range of
subjects, from law to money to
accommodation rights.
Local phone numbers and
addresses in your phone book.
Excellent website:
www.adviceguide.org.uk

Consumer Credit Counselling Service

0800 1381111
www.cccs.co.uk

Inland Revenue Enquiry Centre

For any concern or question
about whether you are paying
too much/too little tax, or to
see if you should be filling in
a tax return, phone your local
IR Enquiry Centre. To find it,
either look in the phone book
under Inland Revenue or visit
their website at:
www.inlandrevenuegov.uk

National Debtline

0808 808 4000
www.nationaldebtline.co.uk

The Site

A brilliant no-nonsense website
for young adults, covering all
sorts of issues. I refer to it
throughout this book.
www.thesite.org

Support4Learning

Information about every
aspect of leaving home –
whether or not you are in
further education.
www.support4learning.org.uk

CheckMyFile

To find out more about
checking your credit rating,
visit:
www.CheckMyFile.com

Accommodation

Contents

Introduction **63**

Different types of accommodation 64
Buying 64
Renting from a private
  landlord 64
Renting from a Housing
  Association 65
Renting through a letting
  agency or estate agent 66
Renting through the local
  council 66
Unfurnished or furnished? 66
What can you afford? 67

**How to find
somewhere to live 68**
What do the ads mean? . . 68
Things you need to find out
 69
Viewing the property 70

References **72**

**Your tenancy
agreement** **73**
Your rights as a tenant . . . 74
Your duties as a tenant . . . 75

Moving in **76**

**Student
  accommodation 78**

**Leaving your
  accommodation 79**

Homelessness **80**

Household bills **81**

**Getting along
together in shared
accommodation 85**
Problems with sharing . . . 85

Troubleshoot **87**

Introduction

You've probably spent the last few years dreaming of having your own place. Does your dream feature a penthouse apartment with a sunken bath and sleek state-of-the-art home entertainment system? Or are you the oldy-worldy cottage type – roses scrambling around the door and a shiny black cat greeting you when you come home each evening? If you're the creative type, you've probably rehearsed colour-schemes far more stylish than your parents' boring ones. Or maybe it's simply the idea of eating noodles with your fingers, leaving the washing-up for the fairies, making as much noise as you want as late as you want as often as you want, and growing four types of mould in a room that no one ever tells you to tidy.

Whichever of these is your inspiration, like most of the really interesting, exciting and worthwhile things in life, achieving that ideal home is not as easy as it seems in dreams. That grim-faced old German philosopher, Nietzsche, had quite a lot to say about things only being worth doing if they are difficult and how the harder they are the greater the pleasure at the end.

Personally, I think he was right. And, certainly, the whole issue of accommodation is riddled with massive potholes to avoid or fall into, but your new home is worth working for. Get it wrong, and it can be one of the greatest sources of stress. Get it right, and you have a safe place to retreat to, relax in, entertain friends in and call your own. If home is where your heart is, your heart has to be in it. If you see what I mean. Nietzsche would probably put it better.

Different types of accommodation

Buying

This is probably not what you are doing straight away. It requires a large amount of money and secure income, even if you take out a hefty loan (mortgage) – and you won't get a mortgage if you aren't earning enough. However, if you are very lucky indeed, you may have financial backing from your family. Helpful parents with spare money – what's that? – might buy a property jointly with you and share responsibility. If so, they will deal with the financial aspects of buying your own place and I don't need to cover it in this book. Phew.

Renting from a private landlord

This includes:

➤ A room in a property which your landlord also lives in – you will be a 'lodger', but still have most of the same rights as any other tenants – though some rules differ slightly, and you should check the contract you are offered by consulting your Citizens Advice Bureau. Contact details in the **Troubleshoot** section ➡ page 87.

➤ A room in a property owned by a landlord who does not live in it, perhaps with the property being shared by several people. You share bathroom and kitchen facilities with the other tenants, as well as washing-up and cleaning, etc. You either make the rules amongst yourselves, or your landlord decides the rules for sharing, etc. This house may be classed as:

• A House in Multiple Occupation (HMO) – this is a

complicated area and the rules about what is and isn't
an HMO are changing and are different in different
parts of the country. At the time of writing this, an
HMO is a property where five or more separate people
(i.e. not related or partners) live and share facilities.
(Different parts of the country may require more
occupants for it to be an HMO.) However, a new
housing bill plans to change this so that an HMO will
be a property shared by two or more unrelated people.
There are some slightly different rules about tenancy
rights in HMOs, so you should check with a Citizens
Advice Bureau if you think you are in one. An HMO
landlord may have to follow more strict rules for health
and safety, such as extra fire regulations.

• A property which only you live in (obviously more
expensive). If you rent a property and then let people
pay to stay in it with you – which is called 'sub-letting'
– you may well be breaking the rules of your tenancy
agreement, so don't plan to do this without checking
the agreement. Also, if you receive money in this way,
you should declare it and pay tax on it. Complicated.
Don't go there without very good advice.

Renting from a Housing Association

A Housing Association is a group of people who come together
with the aim of providing quality low cost houses for rent and
for sale. They get government grants and loans from banks to
build or improve houses and they then rent (or sell) them to people who need them. Some HAs only rent to particular groups,
for example people with learning difficulties. Others simply rent
to people in the greatest need. That might easily be you. Ask
your local council for details of any schemes in your area – contact details in the **Troubleshoot** section ➥ page 87.

Renting through a letting agency or estate agent

More expensive because you may have to pay a fee when they find you somewhere, but has the advantage that it's easier to deal with a problem if it arises. Ask to see a copy of the agreement and take it away to study it *before* you sign anything. Don't sign if you aren't sure, and don't hand over any money before understanding your rights. Check that they are members of one of these organizations: Association of Residential Letting Agencies, National Association of Estate Agents, Royal Institute of Chartered Surveyors, National Approved Letting Scheme.

Renting through the local council

There will be a waiting-list and certain people will get priority, such as pregnant women or families with young children. If you can't find anywhere to live, your local council has a duty to house you if you ask. However, if you are low down their list of priorities, don't expect them to offer you a palace – they have to look after people in greatest need first.

Unfurnished or furnished?

Whoever your landlord is, the property will be either:

➤ **Unfurnished** – cheaper, but you obviously have to buy everything you need, which is definitely not cheap, unless you can sleep on the floor and eat off paper – a perfect excuse for eating noodles with fingers.

➤ **Furnished** – more usual at your stage. You can still start to buy some of your own things. Some rental properties will have the bare minimum of furniture – when you go to view it, think about whether you will need to buy anything else yourself (you could also ask if the landlord would consider providing something else which you regard as essential, but there's no obligation on a landlord to do this. However, it can't be called 'furnished' if it doesn't have the obvious necessities, such as fridge, cooker, plates/cutlery/pans etc., beds, chairs, tables, wardrobes and some shelving.

What can you afford?

You will obviously need to work this out before viewing properties. ➡ the section on **Budgeting**, page 51, for a list of all the costs you need to consider when setting a budget. Unfortunately, nearly everything comes to more than you'll think.

It's also worth remembering that different parts of the country have widely differing council tax charges and also differing service charges for those in council properties. You need to budget for this when considering what rent you can afford.

How to find somewhere to live

Once you've decided which *type* of accommodation you want and can afford, look in:

➤ local newspapers;

➤ student accommodation office;

➤ newsagents – this can be the best place to find somewhere;

➤ noticeboards in local library and shops;

➤ estate agents and letting agencies;

➤ friends who rent – their landlord may know someone else who has a room free;

➤ websites.

What do the ads mean?

vgc	very good condition – by whose standards?
n/s	non-smoking
gdo	good decorative order – yeah, we believe you…
CH/GCH	central heating/gas central heating
bsmt	basement – some basement flats have beautiful sunshine pouring through the windows; others are damp dungeons fit for trolls

Remember, no advert will actually say, 'Poky dmp rat-infestd cellr in dngrous ganglnd area with no st-lights, 4 miles fr nearst bs-stop. No gas sfety certs. Wreckd by prev tnants & stll stnkng of urine/vmt. Prob hauntd by ghst of rcnt mrdr vctm.' Prepare for disappointment. And you may be pleasantly surprised. Or not.

Things you need to find out

Then, start phoning. Here are the things you need to find out *before* you consider visiting the accommodation. But don't ask these questions aggressively – if you decide it sounds promising, you don't want to put your landlord off by sounding like a stroppy serial moaner. You are, in effect, interviewing each other and you both need to trust each other. Everyone wants a quiet life – well, some people don't actually, and they're the ones to watch out for when it comes to signing legal documents.

➤ Exactly where is it? Close to bus route/station/shops/ your place of work?

➤ How many others share the property? Are they male or female (if this matters to you)?

➤ Is it smoking or non-smoking?

➤ Is it furnished or unfurnished? What's the furnishing like? Stinking and stained? Propped up on empty paint-cans?

➤ What's the kitchen like? This and the bathroom can be the clearest indicators of the state of the house and the people in it. Does it look as though you'd get five unpleasant diseases before the first week was up?

➤ Does the central heating work? Is there a radiator in 'your' room? How expensive is it to run? Is there a grubby plastic container beneath it to catch drips?

➤ If you and one or more friends are looking to share together, will you or the landlord be responsible for finding a new tenant if someone leaves? It is best to have individual tenant's agreements, so that if one leaves, the others are not responsible for the extra rent until a new tenant is found.

➤ Would you be a tenant or a licensee? In the past, many landlords have used a licence instead of a tenancy agreement or contract. This gave fewer rights and is now frowned upon. Ask yourself (and the landlord!) why a proper tenancy agreement is not being offered.

➤ How much deposit is required? This is a *one-off* amount which the landlord asks for on top of the rent before you start living there. It is supposed to cover things like damage, or to compensate him/her if you run off owing money. It is usually roughly equal to one month's rent and must be returned to you when you leave, provided you have not caused any damage or broken the terms of your contract. (➡ **Your tenancy agreement** on page 73.)

➤ Does your landlord sound decent? No, you don't actually *ask* this – you use your instincts. And when/if you go to view the property, use your instincts too.

Viewing the property

Keep your eyes open when you visit the property. Better to go with someone else and also take a list of the questions you want to ask. Ask yourself:

➤ Does it look in general good condition?

➤ Does it feel like a secure area? What would it be like walking home at night? How far is it to the bus stop?

➤ Are you near enough to a reasonable shop?

➤ Are the window and door locks in good repair? Do they exist?

➤ How would you get out in a fire? Can you open the windows? Very important – people have been trapped in fires inside double-glazed houses, because they couldn't open the windows. Double glazing can be very hard to smash.

➤ Inside, is it clean, tidy, roomy enough, well-equipped?

➤ Is there anything that bothers you – damp, filthy carpets, grotty furniture? Could you live with it? You may well have to lower your standards after the relatively cushy life you may have had at home.

➤ Can the landlord show you the gas and electrical safety certificates? A landlord *must* renew the gas certificate every year. The rules about electrical certificates vary, depending on the type of property, but there should still be a certificate. Are you happy with how recent it is?

➤ Are there smoke detectors and a carbon monoxide detector in every room where there is a gas appliance? The landlord is not obliged to provide them, but a sensible landlord who cares about the property (and the tenants) should.

➤ Are there any other rules, such as whether you can have a friend to stay the night?

➤ What about the other tenants, if any? You should meet them. Do you think you will get on with them? What sort of system for bills/food/noise/sharing do they have? Do they smile at you? Do they smile at you too much? Remember: you will have to live with them on a daily basis. And nightly. Weekly. Monthly. Year… You get the point? Yes, it's time to be careful and objective.

References

Most landlords nowadays will want a reference to show that you are the wonderful person you say you are. If this is your first rental, you won't have a reference from a previous landlord, but an employer, teacher/tutor, or other decent person will do (not that I'm saying that all employers/teachers/tutors are decent people, but you know what I mean). A reference from your granny won't do, though she is doubtless very decent indeed. If the person giving the reference is a doctor or lawyer, this seems to go down well, even though there are doctors or lawyers whom you wouldn't even want to look after your goldfish, let alone guarantee the safety of your house.

You might also have to provide a bank reference (and you may have to pay a bank charge for this). If your bank account is particularly unhealthy or you've only had it for about five minutes, this isn't going to work very well. In this case, plan A is to tell (and prove to) the landlord how much you earn, as long as that is not too pathetic an amount. Plan B is to persuade a parent or other relative or adult to be the guarantor – this means that if you can't pay, the landlord can get the money from the guarantor instead.

Your tenancy agreement

As I mentioned above, it's better to make sure that this does not use the word 'licence' or call you a licensee. It should be a proper tenancy agreement or contract, and you should be referred to as a tenant.

You should also read the tenancy agreement slowly and carefully. Do not be hurried by an eager landlord thrusting a pen into your hand. It should contain the following information:

➤ What type of rental is this? It could be a 'Fixed term Assured Shorthold Tenancy Agreement' of perhaps six or nine months. 'Fixed term' means that you are committed for that period and if you leave you would be responsible for the rent till the end of the period – though you could find another suitable tenant, with your landlord's agreement. The 'assured' part means that you have full tenant's rights. Another common type of tenancy is an 'Assured Tenancy' without the 'fixed term' part – this means that you will be able to stay for as long as you don't break the terms of the contract. If you are unsure about anything in your contract, ask your local Citizens Advice Bureau (in your phone book).

➤ The amount of rent and how often and how it is collected. Cash? Cheque? Direct debit/standing order? Masked highwayman?

➤ How much notice do you have to give when you want to leave? How much notice does the landlord have to give you?

➤ In what circumstances will the landlord not return your deposit when you leave?

➤ What you are *allowed* to do in terms of putting pictures/mirrors up, decorating, making improvements.

➤ What repairs/decoration/maintenance the landlord will be responsible for.

➤ What bills you are responsible for and how they are paid. (➡ Gas, electricity, water, council tax, sewage, insurance and television – all are explained more fully on page 81.) Find out what the amounts of all these bills have been during the previous year.

➤ Any extra charges.

NOTE: The landlord is responsible for the insurance of the *building* (though the cost will be passed onto you through the rent). This covers things that happen to the roof, walls, ceilings, windows, doors, etc. and permanent fittings such as the bath/sinks. However, the contents, or movable items, will not be covered by this. The landlord should organize insurance for the items that belong to him, but you will need to think about insuring your own items (➡ page 46).

Your rights as a tenant

➤ To live in your home without being harassed by your landlord – harassment would include turning up at midnight to read your meter. Landlords cannot turn up and enter the property without asking your permission beforehand, whether or not you are in the house – though they may obviously hold a key.

➤ Your rent cannot increase more than once a year (for Assured Tenancies).

➤ You can usually only be evicted by a court order, though you can be asked to leave, with proper notice (as stated in your agreement). However, it's different if you share the house or part of the house with the landlord – it is easier to be evicted in this case, though you still have rights. Check with your CAB.

➤ You are allowed to know the address of your landlord.

➤ You have the right to 'quiet enjoyment' of your property. It's your home, even though you don't own it. Paying rent gives you rights.

➤ Your landlord must keep these things in good working order (*whatever* it says in the agreement): water, gas and electricity meters/mains switches and the boiler; toilets/baths/showers/basins/sinks; fires, wall heaters and radiators, whether from the central heating or not. A gas cooker must be safe (and have been tested each year).

Your duties as a tenant

Unfortunately, you have duties too. If all tenants behaved badly, no one would ever become a landlord, and then there'd never be anywhere to rent. Your duties are to:

➤ Look after the property. This means that if you notice a fault or damage, you must tell the landlord, and you must not cause damage. This includes items in the property, such as the fridge or oven – anything that belongs to the landlord.

➤ Pay your rent on time. You must *not* hold back some rent, even if the landlord has annoyed you or not carried out a repair – this would mean that you had broken your agreement and you could be evicted.

➤ Be *reasonable* about letting the landlord come into the property to inspect or repair – after all, how can he/she keep it in good order otherwise?

➤ Ensure that you (and any visitors) do not disturb or annoy the neighbours.

➤ Do everything you agreed to in the tenancy agreement.

Moving in

So, you've decided to go for it and you've signed on the dotted line. Congratulations – you've got a new home. There are a few things to do when you move in:

> ➤ Get the landlord to meet you at the property.
> ➤ Ask the landlord to show you how to work all appliances and give you the instruction booklets where possible.
> ➤ Ask the landlord to show you where the meters and mains switches are (➡ pages 124–30).
> ➤ Make sure you have the landlord's telephone number.
> ➤ There should be an inventory – a list of every item in the place, with a note of any damage. Go through this together and *both* sign it. This is *very* important – it also requires a certain amount of guts to stand there counting teaspoons with a hatchet-faced landlord pretending to be offended because you don't trust him.
> ➤ Take photos of any damage or stains, especially on carpets or walls – and set your camera to print the date if possible. Get them developed immediately and then ask the landlord to sign them. Again, some guts are required for this – but I suggest you smile sweetly and say that your parents are both paranoid neurotics and it was their idea and couldn't the landlord please just humour them? Either that or that you have been reading this amazing book called *The Leaving Home Survival Guide* and the author is a paranoid neurotic and...
> ➤ Check the meter readings together for gas and electricity (and water, if there is one).
> ➤ Get a receipt for the money you hand over – i.e. the

deposit and first month's rent (or week if it's weekly, but monthly is more usual). If you pay weekly, the landlord *must* give you a rent-book, which should be signed each week. If monthly, it's still a good idea to have a rent-book, but not compulsory.

➤ If you are paying by direct debit/standing order, your landlord should have a form for you. Paying by direct debit/standing order is a good idea if you have a bank account, ➡ page 36.

➤ Say goodbye to your landlord and keep your fingers crossed for a very happy and successful rental. Shut the door and do a dance of delight. But not if your new flatmates/housemates are watching.

> **WARNING:** On your first night, you have a boring but quite possibly life-saving job to do: check that you know how to work the window and door locks in your room and around the house. Make sure that all the window keys are near the windows (but not in sight of a burglar's beady eyes).

✱ TIP: Need help with paying the rent? ➡ the **Benefits** section, page 58.

Student accommodation

If you are a student, for at least your first year you will probably live in university 'halls' (not halls at all, really – perfectly ordinary rooms with perfectly ordinary furniture).

Advantages

➤ It should be safe – there are usually lots of people around, and it's run by people whose job it is to look after your safety and welfare.

➤ You don't have to worry about maintenance and repairs (though you still have a responsibility to look after things).

➤ It's sociable – the best way to make a large number of friends in your first year.

Disadvantages

➤ You have no control over your environment, apart from your own room.

➤ It can be noisy and you may not have much privacy.

➤ Some student halls are in serious need of refurbishment – or knocking down.

➤ Students have a reputation for being slovenly creatures who grow unpleasant fungi in milk cartons and do not know what washing-up liquid or the hours of darkness are for. This reputation is quite often accurate.

All accommodation problems will be dealt with by your student accommodation officer. And if you can't work out where to find him or her, you don't deserve to be at university.

Leaving your accommodation

When you leave your rented accommodation, think about the people who will live there after you. A decent citizen leaves the place clean and tidy. Do you really think someone else wants to sweep up your nail-clippings?

You should:

➤ Leave the place as you found it – clean stains from carpets, clean the bathroom and kitchen particularly, clean behind furniture.

➤ Report any damage, whether it was your fault or not – if it was normal wear and tear (for example, a ten-year-old sofa can't be expected to look like a new one), you should not have to pay; if something broke while you were using it, you should.

➤ Get your deposit back from the landlord. Remember those photos that I told you to take in a paranoid neurotic moment on page 76? Aren't you glad you followed my advice? Now you won't have to argue with the landlord about the return of your deposit...

➤ Remove all your own rubbish.

➤ Arrange for your post to be redirected – the GPO will do this for a fee, or you could leave some labels for someone to redirect your post (you do not need stamps for this as it is free).

➤ If your name was on any of the bills (for example gas, electricity, phone), tell the companies that you are leaving – give them some warning. If you pay a share of the bills, take a meter reading when you leave. Leave money for your share of any bills.

Homelessness

If you think that the only homeless people are the ones you might see wrapped in a blanket on the street, think again. Here are some more examples of how you might be considered legally homeless:

➤ You are staying with a friend and sleeping on their floor/sofa.

➤ You have somewhere to live but you are frightened to live there because of harassment or other danger.

➤ The place where you live is unsafe/overcrowded/unsuitable to live in and you can't find anywhere to move to.

➤ You are going to be evicted in the next 28 days and have nowhere to go.

If any of these things apply to you, there are several organizations who are there to help you:

➤ Local council housing office – the council is obliged to try to help you if you are having problems finding suitable, safe accommodation.

➤ Shelter – this is a charity which helps people who are homeless AND anyone having problems with accommodation, even if not homeless. ➡ Contact details in **Troubleshoot** on page 87. They run offices called Housing Aid Centres.

➤ Foyer Federation – another UK-wide charity. ➡ Contact details in **Troubleshoot**.

Household bills

Bills, the boring part of leaving home. Boring but unavoidable. Here are the things you have to pay for, somehow, whether you rent or own, whether you share or not:

Utility bills

Utilities are:

➤ Gas – someone will come to read your meter, usually every three months ('quarterly').

➤ Electricity – as for gas. Oddly, your gas may be provided by an electricity company and your electricity may be provided by a gas company. It's a funny world.

➤ Telephone – there may be a payphone in the property, in which case you'll get no bills but your calls will probably be more expensive. If it's not a payphone, you'll need to find a clever way to decide who pays what. Most phone companies will provide an itemized bill – ask for this if yours doesn't, and say you'll switch companies if they don't. Calls at weekends and after 6 p.m. at night are cheaper, but you could also phone the phone company and ask about different packages that might work out cheaper for your household. Some packages give you free calls in the evenings and at weekends – though you may pay a monthly fee, it can still work out much cheaper. Some *mobile phone* companies have schemes to cut the costs of your *landline* bills too – ask. Your bill will probably be quarterly.

➤ Water – if there's a meter, you'll be charged for what you use. Remember, a shower uses much less water than a bath. If there's no meter, you'll be charged an annual

water-rate, which also covers sewage, so to speak.
A meter can actually work out cheaper.

Your landlord must tell you the names of the companies that provide these. If you are sharing with other people, you will need to work out how you will divide these bills. You can also pay any of these bills by direct debit, which means everything is done monthly and spread over the year (➡ pages 36–8).

NOTE: Utility bills usually include a 'standing charge' – this is an amount you pay before you've used anything.

Insurance
➡ pages 45–50

Television licence
If you have a TV, you must have a licence. It costs £126.50 per year (in 2005). You can get a form from a post office. If you have more than one television, you only need one licence. However, if several people share a building, paying separate rents, they will each need a separate licence. If you are not sure about this, ask at the post office and explain your situation clearly. The fine for not having a licence is up to £1000.

Council tax
This is based on the value of the property and how many people live in it. In an HMO (➡ pages 64–5), the landlord usually deals with the bill but charges the tenants.

If you are responsible for the council tax bill, tell the local authority of your new address.

If you live in a property on your own, there's a reduction – 25%, or more if you are on benefits. If you are on housing benefit, you will not pay council tax.

If the property is *wholly* occupied by full-time students,

there's usually no council tax charge. Check how your council defines a full-time student – it will depend exactly what sort of course you are on. Note: you must get an exemption certificate from your university and ask where you should take it.

If *one* person is not a student but the others are, the one person counts as a single occupant and has a 25% reduction – but must pay the entire remaining 75%. Expensive!

There are some other rules that apply in certain circumstances – check with your local authority and your landlord to make sure you are paying what you should.

Don't ignore letters from councils!

Rent
Obviously.

Food
Is each tenant going to buy separate food or are you going to share? How ballistic will you be when someone a) finishes all the milk and doesn't buy more or b) eats *your* carefully hoarded tin of tomato soup? Does one of your flatmates have a) expensive tastes or b) an enormous appetite?

Service charge in council properties
Councils charge service charges for some or all tenants. These cover services which benefit your property, such as communal gardening and refuse collection.

If you are having problems with paying bills
There are several things you can do:
> If you have a low income or are claiming Income Support or Jobseeker's Allowance, you can apply for Housing Benefit (➡ page 58).
> Discuss the problem with your fellow tenants – maybe the bills are not being divided fairly.
> Speak to the utility companies and see if there's a

cheaper tariff you could be on. Although they do want your money, they don't want you not to be able to pay.

➤ Economize. Yes, I know, very, very boring, but sometimes very, very necessary. There will be lots of ways you can reduce your expenses – ➡ the section on **Cutting expenses,** page 52.

Getting along together in shared accommodation

For this to work (and it often works brilliantly), you'll all need to agree some ground rules. I can't make the rules as everyone's different and has different likes and dislikes. But you need to decide between yourselves how the following things are going to be worked out or shared, and what rules they need:

➤ Bills – could be divided equally or according to use. Consider a weekly kitty for bills or arrange a budget account with the gas and electricity companies, so you don't have a massive bill at the end of the winter.

➤ Shopping for food and other household stuff like cleaning products.

➤ Cleaning communal areas.

➤ Cooking – shared or separate?

➤ Having guests round – someone else's boyfriend/girlfriend taking up permanent residence and occupying the bathroom all the time is one of the most common causes of irritation. I've been there. I have not forgotten. Twenty-one years and four months later, it still bugs me.

➤ Privacy.

➤ Noise – one person's relaxing dance music is another person's night-time torture.

➤ Security – who will take responsibility for locking up? Remember, if locking up is not done properly, your insurance company need not pay if you are burgled.

Problems with sharing

Smaller groups tend to have fewer problems – three or four sharing works better than six or eight. Problems with sharing accommodation, whether with established friends or strangers, are usually caused by:

> ➤ Poor communication: not being able to tell someone that you find a particular habit incredibly irritating or unacceptable.
> ➤ Selfishness: someone not noticing that a personal habit is incredibly irritating or unacceptable.
> ➤ Intolerance: someone being much too fussy and finding perfectly non-irritating and acceptable things incredibly irritating and unacceptable.
> ➤ Incompatibility: when two or more people with quite different incredibly irritating or unacceptable habits have to live together.

Apart from those conditions, life in the land of shared accommodation is a breeze. Here are my not spectacularly original tips for when things are getting you down:

> ➤ Talk – call a house meeting.
> ➤ Get headphones and earplugs.
> ➤ Leave – but find somewhere else first.

Don't let it get you down if one flat-share doesn't work. Put it down to experience. You will have learnt a lot about yourself and what you can and cannot put up with. Whatever it was that got you down this time, make sure that your next place avoids those pitfalls. And it may well not have been your fault – you can't control how other people are.

Good luck in your new home!

Troubleshoot

There are lots of organizations and charities who are waiting for you to call them for help or advice. The advice is free.

As with other aspects of life covered in this book, different parts of the UK may have some different rules or systems. This applies particularly to accommodation.

Citizens Advice Bureau (CAB)

www.adviceguide.org.uk and your phone book.

Landlord-Law

Advice for landlords *and* tenants at www.landlordlaw.co.uk

Shelter

For all housing problems, not only homelessness. If there is a Housing Advice Centre in your region, you will find it under 'Shelter' in your phone book. http://www.shelternet.org.uk
    Shelterline is the free advice line for people at risk of homelessness: 0808 800 4444

Local Authority Housing Office/ Department

If you don't know the full name of your local council/authority, look under 'council' in the phone book.

Students

Your university accommodation office/officer.

National Union of Students

www.nusonline.co.uk

The Site

This wonderful website has lots of info. about accommodation issues: www.thesite.org

In the home

Contents

Introduction **93**

Cleaning **94**
Cleaning and the
   environment 94

Cleaning clothes . . . **96**
Laundry symbols 96
Washing powder/liquid . .97
Drying clothes 98
At the laundrette 99
Dry-cleaning 100

**Cleaning around the
house** **101**
Detergents/disinfectants/
   bleach 102
Vacuum cleaners 103
A word about sheets 103
A word about kitchen cloths
  104
Removing stains – carpets,
   sofas and clothing 104
Wine stains 105
Special plea about chewing-
   gum 106
How often should you clean?
  107

**DIY – household
repairs and minor
improvements**   **108**
Adopt a practical adult . .108
Essential tools 109
Replacing a light bulb . . .109
When a fuse 'blows' 111
Overloaded sockets 114
When a household item goes
   wrong 114
Putting nails or screws in
   walls or doors 115
Screws in solid plaster walls
  115
Screws in hollow
   plasterboard walls 116
Where can you *not* put a nail
   or screw? 117
How are you supposed to
   know where wires or pipes
   are? 117
Using an electric drill 117
Unblocking a sink 119
Descaling a shower head (or
   kettle) 120
Removing mildew from the
   edge of shower/bath/sink
  120

3

IN THE HOME

Filling small cracks or holes
..................121
Painting 121

Mains switches and taps – electricity, water and gas ...124

Electricity 124
Electricity meter 125
Water 125
Water leak 127
A dripping tap 127
Airlocks in radiators 128
Toilets 128
Water meter 129
Frozen pipes 129
Gas 130

Pest control 131

Calling in the experts 132

Safety in the home 135

Security 135
Going away? 135
Fire 136
Carbon monoxide poisoning
...................136
Electricity 137
Gas 138
Danger points in the house
...................138

Chemical-free living 139

Troubleshoot 141

3

IN THE HOME

Introduction

Before you left home, you almost certainly lost no sleep over what would happen if a pipe burst or the electricity failed. Don't lose any sleep now either – just locate the relevant taps or switches as you read this chapter, and then sleep soundly. The time to find your water mains tap is not when jets of freezing water are shooting from under the sink with a terrifying hissing sound. Nor is that the time to discover that not all water pipes come from the mains anyway. The time to know these things is now.

Whether you are a tenant or a home owner, you have to look after the property you live in. It's your duty, but it also makes your home safer and more comfortable for you. If you are a tenant or in university accommodation, some of the things in this chapter are the responsibility of your landlord or the university. Find out from them what you *can* or *must* do, and what you *may not* or *do not have* to do. You should read the chapter on **Accommodation** (➡ especially pages 74–5) for more about rights and responsibilities.

IN THE HOME

Cleaning

Boring but necessary. I am not going to descend to the level of telling you how to use a vacuum cleaner or duster. I am just going to pick out some things you might not know and which might help you not wreck your or your landlord's precious, or not-so-precious, possessions.

Actually, I do have something to say about dust: ➡ page 101.

Cleaning and the environment

Unfortunately, many modern cleaning products contain extremely strong chemicals, chemicals which your body may absorb and the residues of which end up in your house and/or flushed away into the water system and environment. The extent to which we are exposed to such chemicals on a daily basis is only now being fully realized. As young people, you are often better than us older ones at looking at the way what we do affects our environment, but you may be less good at focusing on future damage to your bodies. But avoiding chemicals where possible makes perfect sense for both reasons.

You may have watched the recent television series, 'How Clean is Your Home?' Apart from being the most irritating piece of television that I have ever witnessed, this programme did contain excellent advice about cheap, effective and environmentally brilliant ways of cleaning all sorts of things around the house – methods which could positively affect the environment, your health, and your bank balance. I recommend the book. It avoids the necessity of listening to the presenters.

I also recommend you search out a product called Spotless.

There are other similar things. They are natural, biodegradable, non-acid pastes and are brilliant. Spotless is very like something I remember my mother using – it was called Gumption in those days. It is recommended for enamel, porcelain, china, ovens, cookware, sinks and baths, most floors, vinyl and plastic.

Also ➥ the section **Chemical-free living** on page 139.

Cleaning clothes

Laundry symbols
(usually on a label in a side seam, or at the neck)

 handwash only

   machine wash at this temperature (30 is quite cool, 40 is warm, 60 is hot)

 machine wash on 'delicates' cycle (at temp. shown)

   three spots on the iron means hot iron, one spot means very cool

 may be dry-cleaned

 must not be dry-cleaned

 may be tumble-dried

 must not be tumble-dried

There may be other instructions. For example, it might say 'wash as wool' – a washing machine will show a wool setting, so use it. This is a more gentle setting than 'delicates'. If you wash things at a hotter or more vigorous wash than recommended, you'll end up with clothes that look as though they were made for misshapen dolls.

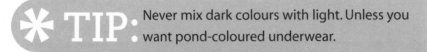

TIP: Never mix dark colours with light. Unless you want pond-coloured underwear.

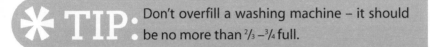

TIP: Don't overfill a washing machine – it should be no more than $^2/_3$ – $^3/_4$ full.

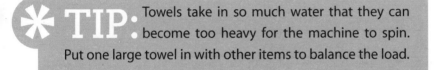

TIP: Towels take in so much water that they can become too heavy for the machine to spin. Put one large towel in with other items to balance the load.

3

IN THE HOME

Washing powder/liquid

➤ 'Automatic' – designed for use in a washing machine. Don't try using this for handwashing.

➤ 'For delicates/woollens' – this may be for a machine or for hand-washing, so you'll need to check. There is no need to have separate powder/liquid for delicates/woollens that go in a machine, but you will need something for handwashing garments that can't go in a machine; usually a liquid.

➤ 'Biological' – contains an enzyme (type of chemical, for those of you who have already forgotten your chemistry) which is designed to work on stains.

➤ 'Non-biological/non-bio' – does not contain enzymes and therefore more environmentally friendly and perhaps kinder for sensitive skin. I never notice any difference in cleaning ability between bio and non-bio.

➤ 'Sensitive/hypo-allergenic' – may be better if you suffer from eczema/allergies.

➤ Special products for coloured clothes/white clothes? Not really necessary, in my opinion, though of course the manufacturers want you to have different products for everything. They'll probably invent something specially for Tuesdays soon.

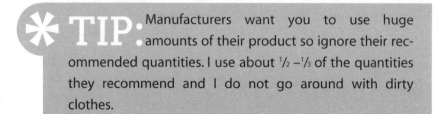

TIP: Manufacturers want you to use huge amounts of their product so ignore their recommended quantities. I use about ½ –⅓ of the quantities they recommend and I do not go around with dirty clothes.

Drying clothes

The best way to dry clothes is outside in the sunshine, pegged to the line and flapping in the breeze like happy ghosts. (➡ **Chemical-free living** on page 139.) But what if you don't have an outside, or sunshine, and it's raining? Or if you're sick of hanging the washing out in the morning in ultra-efficient manner, disappearing off to work/college/play, and realizing halfway through the day that hurricane Nora has hit town and that your washing is likely to be spread over the neighbour's organic vegetable patch?

If you have a tumble-dryer, it's time to use it. But be careful, drying clothes is not as trouble-free as it might seem. First of all, some clothes can't be tumble-dried – this is the symbol for something that must *not* be tumble-dried: ⊠ Ignore this only if you want your best jumper to be fit only for a deformed doll.

Secondly, you cannot dry a whole washing machine load at the same time: you need to dry the light-weight things first, such as shirts and pillowcases; then heavier things like socks and thick rugby shirts. As for towels, well, how long have you got?

Thirdly, because tumble-dryers use a lot of electricity and often take a long time (especially if you insist on putting towels in them), they are not an eco-friendly option.

Your other option is to hang your clothes on an airer (a cheap folding contraption available from big supermarkets or DIY/household shops), or on radiators, or in an airing-cupboard if you have one. And wait. Position the airer in the warmest part of the house, somewhere airy, not in a dank cellar, and not near cooking food.

Do *not* hang clothes to dry anywhere near an open fire or electric fire.

Whatever you choose as your drying option, do it as soon as you take the clothes from the washing machine. If you leave them screwed up in a basket – or screwed up anywhere for that matter – you will have a stinking mass of mouldy material before you can say 'Why didn't school teach me anything useful?'

At the laundrette

These are not nearly as scary as they look. Forget 'Eastenders' and fierce nicotine-ingrained women or dramatic murders – they're not going to happen. Probably. Just go in and ask someone what to do – it's really that simple. If there's someone on duty, you can ask for a 'service wash' – this is when you pay the staff to do it for you. Otherwise, ask:

➤ How long will it take?
➤ How do I know how much I can put in?
➤ What about drying – how much does it cost and how long will it take?

You don't have to wait around while your clothes wash themselves. You can go and do something useful, or you can sit and read a book and hope that someone very interesting will come in.

✳ TIP: You can buy washing powder in the laundrette but it will be very expensive. Bring your own.

✳ TIP: If you walk to the laundrette, and if you do not use a tumble-dryer, your clothes will weigh *much* more on the way back…

✳ TIP: Whether using a laundrette or your own washing machine: First sort machine-washable clothes into dark colours and white/lights. In each group, find the item which needs the coolest/most delicate wash and wash the whole wash at that setting.

Dry-cleaning

Dry-cleaning is very expensive – try not to buy too many clothes which say dry-clean only. Clean them rarely – instead, sponge a spot with a slightly damp sponge and a little soap (but test an invisible area first to make sure the colour doesn't fade). You can also buy a dry-cleaning solvent, which will have instructions on it – very useful for spots or marks but not for cleaning a whole garment.

Cleaning around the house

I said I was going to say something about dust. Take a deep breath (but not too deep if your house is dusty) and read on. It used to be said that dust never harmed anyone. Unfortunately, the person who said this was a) badly-informed and b) a wishful thinker. Ordinary house dust contains a cocktail of up to 180 chemicals, including many which are known to be either carcinogenic (cancer-causing), or damaging to the immune system, the reproductive system, or the hormone (endocrine) system. These chemicals particularly collect in carpets, turning a simple piece of floor covering into a toxic wasteland. (➡ **Chemical-free living** on page 139.)

Even apart from the long-term invisible damage dust could be doing to you, if you have asthma it's most likely that house-dust will make you worse, and asthma is a serious condition which can occasionally be fatal.

Finally, if you leave dust lying there, it mixes with grease and moisture in the air and is much harder to remove. It is actually better to do it quickly and often, unless you actually *like* getting down on your hands and knees and scrubbing.

Some surfaces are best dusted using a spray polish – look at the instructions on the can to see which ones, but examples would be wood and mirrors. Others are perfectly easily dealt with using a damp cloth – painted surfaces and skirting-boards are examples. Natural (unvarnished) wood benefits from sometimes being treated with good quality furniture polish – if you have inherited Aunt Mabel's antique coffee table, her ghost will smile happily on you if you do this.

Detergents/disinfectants/bleach

Remember – all these products end up in the environment, so the less you use the better.

Detergent

Designed to cut through grease and dirt. Washing-up liquid is an example of a detergent. Detergent doesn't kill bacteria but by using hot water to help it wash away the dirt, most dirt disappears, taking most bacteria along with it. Some washing-up liquid says 'anti-bacterial': don't rely on it killing bacteria as efficiently as a proper disinfectant. .

Disinfectant

Designed to kill at least most bacteria. You usually dilute it – read the instructions. Good for hard floors, kitchens and bathrooms. Some disinfectants are designed to be used on human skin, for cuts and grazes; others are not – again, read the instructions.

Anti-bacterial spray

A type of disinfectant which you do not need to dilute with water. Can be sprayed directly onto a kitchen side, for example. Will do a pretty good job of killing many germs, if used according to instructions.

Bleach

Kills all relevant germs dead. However, you have to be careful – a tiny splash will remove the colour from clothing or carpets and you will never remove the stain. Use neat (undiluted) down toilet bowls. Dilute in water to clean and disinfect a kitchen floor.

Bleach is great for removing stains from anything white: a white sink, bath, shower-tray, tile grouting (the cement stuff between tiles). On non-white kitchen sides it will also remove stains of things like curry and it is brilliant for removing the dirt from grime-stained kitchen floors. Some materials will be damaged by it or will fade, so do check with the manufacturer or try a test on an invisible bit first. Don't use it on wood or metal.

> **!** **WARNING:** If you buy a kitchen cleaner, notice whether it says 'contains bleach'. If it does, it will do a great cleaning job but you'll need to be careful not to get it on clothes.

> **!** **WARNING:** Bleach and bleach products should not touch your skin – if they do, wash immediately in plenty of water. Always wear rubber gloves.

> **✳ TIP:** In the kitchen, you will find that some surfaces get a horrible greasy coat on them. Buy a product that says 'cuts through grease' and use a sponge with a scouring pad. Put your rubber gloves on, turn the radio up, and get scrubbing. Otherwise, it looks disgusting, feels foul every time you touch it, and attracts flies and bacteria.

Vacuum cleaners

Empty the bag often (unless you are lucky enough to have one that doesn't need a bag at all). Nearly all vacuum cleaners lose most of their power once the bag is $1/3$ full.

A word about sheets

Brace yourself for this information: you sweat during the night and shed skin. Lots of it. If you just have one sheet between you and the mattress, the greasy sweat and skin find their way into the mattress, where they become food for bedbugs and take up long-term residence in your mattress. You should have another sheet under the sheet, preferably doubled. This undersheet does not need to be washed every time you wash the other sheets/duvet cover, but do wash it every few weeks. All sheets should be washed at high temperature (preferably 90°C) or the bugs and mites survive. You can buy something called a 'mattress-protector', which serves the same purpose but does it better.

A word about kitchen cloths

A cloth that is used for wiping sides or washing dishes is the playground of millions of nasties – it is the dirtiest place in your kitchen, mainly because a cloth tends to be wet often and then left screwed up, letting the bugs multiply. Regularly soak your cloth overnight in a mild bleach solution and then spread it out to air. For washing-up, it's *much* better to use a nylon brush, not a cloth, and a scouring sponge for caked-on dirt.

Removing stains – carpets, sofas and clothing

Different stains need different treatment, but there are some things that apply to all.

> ➤ Deal with it straight away.
> ➤ Don't push the stain into the carpet/sofa by rubbing.
> ➤ First get rid of excess substance by a) scraping gently with a knife and b) blotting with a dry cloth (e.g. a tea towel or towel).
> ➤ Use the least possible amount of liquid to clean it – otherwise you'll get a water stain.
> ➤ Most spillages respond to a mild solution of washing-up liquid, or other detergent such as soap – but don't use automatic dishwasher detergent and never use anything with bleach in unless you actually *want* to

leave a white mark.

➤ Supermarkets sell a range of excellent carpet stain removers, which can all also be used on sofas, etc.

➤ Before using any substance to remove the stain, test on an area which doesn't show.

Wine stains

A lot of people say that if you spill wine, you should chuck salt on it. Some even sillier people say you should pour white wine on a red wine spillage. In fact, it can be quite amusing at a party watching everyone chuck salt and white wine onto the carpet and arguing about who's right. But not amusing at all if it's your carpet. The truth is that both tricks are pointless. In recent tests conducted by 'wine scientists' (nice work if you can get it), white wine and salt were the least effective methods of all those used. Salt is bad, because when you dye an item you actually use salt to *set* the colour, so all you are going to do is make things worse. White wine is a bad idea because a) the less liquid on the carpet the better b) it's an unforgivable waste of wine. Unless you serve very horrible wine at your parties.

With a level of complete impracticality that you would not expect from wine scientists, they concluded that the best solution is bleach. This is a very silly idea, unless you happen to have an absolutely white carpet, which you certainly don't. No one does.

The best way to remove a wine stain (and many others) from carpets is bicarbonate of soda. Buy it from a supermarket. If the stain is still wet, sprinkle the bicarb. onto the carpet, press in and hoover up. Or if it's already dry, make a solution of several teaspoons of bicarb. in water and dab firmly with a cloth (don't get the carpet too wet).

You can also use soda water – not just carbonated/fizzy water but actual soda water from a siphon or club soda bottle.

There is a wonderful website at www.howtocleananything.com. It will tell you how to remove every stain you can imagine, and several you probably hadn't considered, like acne medication. It even tells you what to do if you get sprayed by a skunk, which is useful.

> **✳ TIP:** If a stain has turned brown, for example from coffee, chocolate or blood, a solution of white wine vinegar (1 part vinegar to 2 parts warm water) will deal with it.

Special plea about chewing-gum

Anyone who drops chewing-gum anywhere is disgusting and doesn't deserve to be your friend. It's people like this who are ruining the look of our streets too – they are litter louts who spoil our country for everyone else. Litter is ugly and the people who cause it are uglier still. There, I've said my piece.

> **✳ TIP:** To remove chewing-gum, freeze it off. Get a piece of ice wrapped in a plastic bag and rub it on the gum till it becomes hard. Ease it off with a knife. Then use a small amount of acetone-based nail polish remover and wipe the residue away with a clean cloth. Rinse well with mild detergent solution.

How often should you clean?

How dirty are you? How clean do you want to be? There are no rules – do what you feel is right. But here are some guidelines anyway, because I like guidelines:

Object/place	Every...
Tea towels	2–3 days – they love germs
Sheets and pillow cases	week
Duvet covers	2 weeks
Duvet	year
Toilet and bathroom	week
Kitchen sides and floor	week (or after spillage)
Kitchen bin	when the bag has leaked (often, in my experience)
Bedroom	7–10 days
Other rooms	whenever they need it – or when visitors are coming and you care what they think
Windows	when you can't see through them
Skirting-boards	when you are ashamed of them

DIY – household repairs and minor improvements

With some of these things, you'll need to check with your landlord to make sure it's OK to do them. This symbol 🐾 means you should check. With simple things, such as replacing a fuse, it's also a good idea to ask your landlord to show you how to do this, so that you can do it yourself.

Adopt a practical adult

You do not want to spend a fortune calling out a tradesperson each time something very tiny goes wrong. My cunning plan is that you identify a nearby adult who seems practical. Someone like me would be ideal; someone like certain other members of my family would not. Think about anyone living nearby – a relative, friend of the family or neighbour. A neighbour coming home laden with carrier bags from a DIY store is a dead giveaway. Target this person with flattery. People do like to be asked for advice. It makes them feel clever and wise.

Once you have ascertained that this person can help, he or she is now your APA – Adopted Practical Adult. APAs can be rewarded by the odd packet of biscuits, or a not-too-cheap bottle of wine if you feel they have been particularly helpful. Mine's a dry white.

I don't want to insult your intelligence, but I have to remind you that you should be careful about inviting strangers into your home, particularly of the opposite sex. Follow your instincts about this and do not take risks. Consider having a friend with you, and if you become in the slightest bit uncomfortable, do not ask this APA in again. Get a new APA.

Essential tools

➤ Three screwdrivers: a large/medium one, a small/tiny one and a 'cross-head' one (sometimes called a 'Philips') – this is one where the tip is in the form of a cross. Some screws are this shape, and an ordinary screwdriver won't work for them;

➤ A hammer;

➤ Assorted screws, nails and carpet tacks;

➤ Assorted fuses (and assorted fuse wire if you live in an older house which does not have a modern fuse-box – ➡ pages 112–13);

➤ Strong glue – not paper glue, but something that mends china, metal and plastic;

➤ There's a wonderful product which you can use instead of nails – it's basically a very strong glue. It will fix something permanently to the wall or pretty much anywhere you choose to put it, as long as the object is not too heavy and can be supported while it dries. It is called, rather unimaginatively, 'No More Nails'.

Replacing a light bulb

You've probably heard all the light bulb jokes, so I'm not going to tell you one here. Suffice to say that they (jokes, not light bulbs) were invented because changing a light bulb is supposed to be the simplest thing in the world. Well, it is, but if you haven't done it before, it doesn't seem simple. The second time you do it will be a doddle.

➤ Make sure the light is switched off at the wall. If you aren't sure, turn the mains electricity off (➡ page 124).

➤ If any part of the fitting looks broken, or if part of the flex/cable looks damaged so you can see the copper wires through it, don't touch it – call an electrician.

➤ Remove the old bulb: some light bulbs simply screw in and out, in which case you hold the fitting in one hand

and use the other hand to unscrew the bulb; but the more usual fitting is called a bayonet fitting (➡ below) and requires a special but still simple method: put one hand firmly above/behind the whole fitting to hold it steady; with the other hand, hold the bulb and push towards the fitting while twisting slightly anti-clockwise till it becomes free. It may be quite stiff. Just keep trying, being bold but careful at the same time. Do not have your face directly underneath – I have never heard of one breaking, but it is theoretically possible.

➤ Examine the top of the bulb (the glass bit) and see whether it is a 40W, or 60W, or 100W. The inside of the shade may also tell you what is required. You should never use a higher wattage than the one recommended for that fitting. You can use a lower one if you want, particularly if you like going round in a murky gloom.

➤ Nowadays, there are umpteen different types of bulb, so you also need to look at the metal part, the part that screws into the fitting. Is it a screw fitting or does it have two tiny prongs sticking out at the side? The two tiny prongs mean it is a 'bayonet' fitting. However, it doesn't stop there, because in either case it could be 'small' or 'standard', and how on earth can you tell if you've got nothing to compare it with? You have two options:

• Take it with you to a shop so you can find one the same.

• Measure it: small is about 1 cm across; standard is about 2.5 cm across.

➤ Push the new bulb into the fitting firmly (you'll feel a slight springiness – push the springiness in) and then twist clockwise. If the bulb stays in, you've done it right; if not, simply try again – you probably didn't push it in firmly enough and were a bit timid. Timid will get you nowhere with light bulbs.

RATHER OBVIOUS WARNING: Don't put your finger inside the light fitting unless the mains is turned off. I have to say these things.

✱ TIP: Keep a stock of all the different bulbs your light fittings require. Don't forget the kitchen and bathroom lights – they'll be irritatingly different. Just take some out and have a look – and by the time you've done that a few times, you will be the world expert on light bulbs. By the way, it only takes one reader of *The Leaving Home Survival Guide* to change…

When a fuse 'blows'

A fuse is a short length of wire which is deliberately thinner than the rest of the circuit, so that if something goes wrong, the fuse 'blows'. This means that it breaks at that thin point, the current stops flowing, danger is prevented, and all you have to do is replace the fuse.

How would I know a fuse has 'blown'?

If an item such as a hairdryer stops working, or if a bedside lamp stops working and still doesn't work when you put a new bulb in, a blown fuse is a likely possibility. It is simple to find out, so worth a try before you get further help or take the item for repair.

How do I do it?

If it's a moveable item, the fuse will be inside the plug. Remove the plug from the socket and use a small screwdriver to remove the cover of the plug by unscrewing the one large screw (usually) underneath it. The fuse is the small cylinder lying between two metal prongs. Prise it out using a screwdriver, and simply replace it with a new fuse of exactly the same 'amp' value. It will tell you this on the fuse. You can buy a packet of assorted fuses very cheaply at most supermarkets, all DIY shops and most decent general stores/convenience shops.

If the item still does not work, unfortunately you have a more serious problem than a fuse. If it's a major item, you may want to ask an electrician or contact the manufacturer's repair-line. A smaller item will probably cost more to repair than it is worth. Whichever, ask your APA first.

Sometimes a fuse might be behind a plastic square on a wall – like a light switch but with no switch. A fixed bathroom heater or shaver point would have this. It's still easy to deal with but you *must* switch off the electricity at the mains (➡ page 124). Then unscrew the plastic cover and replace the fuse, as if it were in a plug.

The final type of fuse blowing is when one whole circuit in the house goes at the same time: if a whole section of the house suddenly has no lights working, or no sockets working, this is what has probably happened. This can happen because an item of equipment is faulty or a light bulb has broken or too many appliances are being used from the same socket at the same time.

In modern houses, or houses which have been fairly recently rewired, this is very simple: find the mains fuse box (➡ page 124). Lift the cover so that you can see the switches properly. These are called 'trip switches' and there will be one for each area of the house. They will be helpfully labelled. You will probably see that one is 'off' – just flick it back on and you should find that the relevant lights or appliance in the affected part of the house come back on.

If you live in an older house which does not have these simple trip switches in the mains fuse box, as long as you have some **fuse wire** in the house, you can still deal with it yourself.

➤ Switch the electricity off at the mains (➡ page 124).
➤ Next to the mains switch, you will see all the mains fuses – these are plastic rectangles about 5 cm tall and 2 cm

across. They should have writing on them to tell you which bit of the house each one is for. Pull out the relevant one firmly and look at the underside of it. You should see that the piece of wire is broken. (If it isn't, make sure that one of the other fuses isn't broken instead. If all seem to be intact, you'll need an electrician.)

➤ Once you've found the broken wire, select a new piece of fuse wire *of the same thickness* and put it in the fuse in exactly the same way that the old one was fixed. If this doesn't seem obvious or you have any doubts, get your APA, landlord or an electrician.

➤ Replace the plastic rectangle.

➤ Switch the mains back on. If the electricity in the relevant part of the house still doesn't work, call an electrician.

If the same trip switch keeps tripping or the same fuse in the mains box keeps blowing, there must be a fault. It may be something simple. Check these things:

➤ Have you put too many items on one socket (i.e. using a multi-way adaptor)? ➡ **Overloaded sockets** on page 114. If so, unplug some and use different sockets.

➤ Is an item faulty and therefore tripping the circuit each time? You can check this:

• Turn the trip switch off, if it isn't already.

• Unplug everything on that circuit (simply switching off is not enough – they must be unplugged).

• Flick the trip switch back on.

• Plug in and switch on one item at a time. When the switch trips again at the main fuse box, you've identified your problem item. You need to think about getting it repaired/checked or binning it.

If you cannot identify the fault and a switch still keeps tripping, call an electrician.

Overloaded sockets

Don't plug too many things into one electrical socket. That's the usual cause of a fuse blowing. Some electrical items use much less power, so some things can combine well without any problems. But do not use more than one of the heaviest power users or more than three of the lighter ones on one socket at the same time.

Heavy power users:
➤ hairdryers
➤ vacuum cleaners
➤ washing machines/tumble-dryers
➤ electric blenders/food processors/mixers
➤ electric heaters or fan heaters

Lighter power users:
➤ lights
➤ stereos/radios
➤ TVs/videos/DVDs
➤ computer components (bear in mind that the monitor and the PC unit have two separate plugs, making them count as two items)

When a household item goes wrong

➤ Switch off and UNPLUG the item before doing anything.
➤ Don't try to unscrew anything unless the manufacturer's handbook says you can.
➤ Remove obvious blockage – e.g. from vacuum cleaner brush.
➤ Read the manufacturer's handbook.
➤ If there is no power/noise at all, check the fuse (➡ pages 111–13).
➤ If none of that helps, phone the manufacturer – and ask about costs before you agree to any repair. Have the model name and serial number handy – usually found underneath or behind the item. Have your receipt handy if it's within its warranty period.

Putting nails or screws in walls or doors

A screw is stronger than a nail. But you cannot put a screw directly into a plaster or brick wall.

Nails – a nail will be fine for hanging a picture or fairly light mirror. Ideally, use picture hooks, which come as single or double – i.e. with one nail or two. If in doubt, choose one with two, as it will be stronger. Knock the nail in at a downward angle. page 117 for **Where can you not put a nail or screw?**

Screws – in wood. You can screw a nail directly into wood – though it *may* make a crack in the wood if you do not drill a hole first. **Using an electric drill** page 117.

If you want to fix something like a small shelf or a screw-in hook to a plaster or brick wall, you will have to become acquainted with nifty little things called wall plugs. The idea is that you drill a hole (with an electric drill), push the wall plug in and then screw your screw or hook into the plastic. This grips it tightly and makes a very strong fixing.

If you live in a very new house, with plasterboard walls (they sound hollow when tapped), welcome to the wonderful world of drill-free screwing and go to the section on **Screws in hollow plasterboard walls** on page 116.

Screws in solid plaster walls

It sounds a bit scary, but learning to do this will be the single most useful and money-saving DIY task you can learn. Here's my advice, based on thousands of successful drillings (and a few less successful ones early on, which is the best way to learn).

➤ At a DIY shop, find a helpful member of staff. Tell
   him/her what you want to put on your wall. Ask what

size screw, wall plug and drill 'bit' (➡ page 117 **Using an electric drill**) you need. (If you are fixing something that came with screws and wall plugs, you won't need to consider these choices, and the instructions will tell you what size drill bit to use.)

➤ Back at home, mark where you want to make the holes (making sure you avoid places where there might be wires/pipes ➡ page 117).

➤ Drill the hole to the depth of the wall plug.

➤ Push the wall plug in till it is level with the surface of the wall – tap gently if necessary, but don't bash with a hammer. If it doesn't go in fairly easily, the hole may not be big enough.

➤ Screw in your screws tightly, fixing the item to the wall.

➤ If it's a mirror, look in it and smile – you just did your first serious DIY.

Screws in hollow plasterboard walls

➤ Off to the DIY store again, this time in search of 'wall plugs for plasterboard walls'. The best ones are the metal ones, but you have to use the screws provided, which *may* not fit the item you want to install. If not, choose the plastic ones. Don't buy 'heavy-duty' ones – that is a job for a professional. You should not attempt to hang something large and heavy until you are an expert driller and know what weights different materials will hold.

➤ Back at home, mark where you want the screws to go – but you *must* choose hollow parts of the wall, so do some tapping till you find suitable spots.

➤ Simply screw the metal (or plastic) wall plug straight into the wall with a cross-head screwdriver till it is level with the surface.

➤ Screw in your screw tightly, fixing the item firmly to the wall.

WARNING: With any drilling into a wall, you can have a problem with the plaster. It can be too soft and crumbly or you can hit a particularly hard bit of wall beneath. In these cases, unfortunately, there are too many and too complicated solutions. I can only suggest you put a poster over the mess and call in the professionals – starting with your APA. It's not your fault – a sensible workman/woman always blames the plaster.

Where can you *not* put a nail or screw?

You can put a nail into woodwork or a wall, but you have to think whether there might be an electric wire or water pipe behind that particular spot. This is not something to joke about, as I know from an expensive, frightening and ultimately embarrassing experience in the days before I became renowned for my DIY prowess.

How are you supposed to know where wires or pipes are?

Electric cables and water pipes follow accepted patterns, unless they were installed by a complete idiot. However, by far the safest thing is to assume that yours might have been installed by a complete idiot and buy a pipe and wire detector from a DIY shop. They are not expensive. I wish I'd had one…

WARNING: Do not put a nail or screw into a window frame – you may hit glass.

Using an electric drill

An electric drill is a fantastically useful piece of equipment and much easier to use than you might think. It also doesn't cost very much and will save you a fortune in calling out impossible-to-find and expensive joiners to do simple things for you. You need:

> ➤ a simple electric drill – you do not need a 'hammer-action' drill unless you plan to get really serious;
> ➤ a circuit-breaker/power-breaker – this is an inexpensive item that you plug into an electric socket; you then plug the drill (or anything else) into the circuit-breaker. This gives you complete safety in case something goes wrong – it cuts the electric current instantly;
> ➤ a selection of different widths of drill 'bit'. A bit is the bit which actually makes the hole. There are different bits for wood or for masonry (walls). Your drill will probably come with a selection of all the most common ones and you may never need any others;
> ➤ an extension cable – an electric drill usually comes with a very short cable, fine if you happen to want to drill something a few inches from an electric plug, but hopeless otherwise. An extension lead/cable costs very little – make sure it is designed for the same power as (or greater than) your drill, which you can do by comparing the wattage or voltage on your drill with that given on the extension.

✱ TIP: Practise drilling into places that don't matter, so that you get the feel of it. The most common problem at first is holding it steady so you drill in the exact place you want.

! WARNING: If you have to stand on something, be *very* careful. Only stand on a chair or step-ladder if it is completely steady. Do not use near water or a gas fire. Wear strong shoes as well, preferably rubber-soled. Use common sense and follow all the safety instructions that come with the drill.

Unblocking a sink

If a sink, bath or shower seems to be draining very slowly, or not at all, you have a blockage. There are various ways to deal with this before resorting to a plumber. Nine times out of ten, you'll be able to deal with it yourself.

There are chemical products you can buy to deal with blockages. They are very, very strong, which is good and bad. Good because they sometimes work, bad because if you use the wrong one for the wrong type of pipe, they will damage the pipe. They are also exceptionally environmentally unfriendly. And pretty expensive.

Here are some better methods:

Method A – bicarbonate of soda (or caustic soda, which is sometimes called washing soda)

➤ Remove visible gunge with a piece of coat-hanger wire.
➤ Pour boiling water down.
➤ Wearing strong rubber gloves, pour bicarbonate of soda down.
➤ Follow this with more boiling water.
➤ You may have to repeat this a few times.

Method B – the plunger
➤ Buy a cheap, old-fashioned plunger.
➤ Run hot water into the sink until it would cover the bottom of the plunger.
➤ Place plunger over plughole.
➤ Cover the overflow vent with a damp cloth.
➤ Firmly press plunger up and down and enjoy the gloopy noise it makes.
➤ Watch disgusting debris come rising up to meet you.

It's a very good idea to pour boiling water and bicarbonate of soda down sinks every now and then as prevention.

For a blockage that will not respond to these methods, call a plumber.

Descaling a shower head (or kettle)

In some areas, water contains lime, which builds up as limescale on the insides of kettles and shower heads, for example. It is a crusty white residue. Vinegar is a simple and cheap way to deal with this – simply unscrew the offending shower head and clean with a white vinegar and water solution. (But be careful – if the shower head has a layer of 'plating' on it, too strong a vinegar solution, or soaking it, could damage this shiny plating). You can also put a cup of vinegar in the kettle and boil it – but make sure you rinse it all away before your housemates make tea…

If you let limescale build up on the shower head, you can eventually cause problems with the hot water system.

> **!** **WARNING:** You can remove limescale from other things with vinegar, but be careful with plated taps (e.g. gold-plated ones): use a weak solution and rinse off well and quickly. Do not put vinegar on marble or veneered surfaces. Remember: vinegar is an acid.

Removing mildew from the edge of shower/bath/sink

Neat bleach is the answer. I've never found anything else that works, though I'd love someone to prove me wrong. Also, do it when the mould stain isn't too bad – the longer you leave it, the harder it will be.

If the grouting (cement between tiles) has gone discoloured, you can buy a special tile-whitener that you paint on. Fiddly but effective. Trouble is, all the rest of the grouting immediately looks dingy and you'll end up doing the whole lot.

Filling small cracks or holes

Plastering large cracks or holes is definitely a job for an expert, but anyone can deal with small cracks.

Cracks in walls

You need:

➤ a tube or pot of ready-to-use instant filler, available from any DIY store and some large supermarkets. Do not buy 'flexible' filler. Check the label to see if it's suitable for what you want it for;

➤ a small item called a flexible filler knife.

Simply follow the instructions on the pot/tube.

Cracks beside edge of bath/shower/sink

You need:

➤ a tube of ready-to-use flexible filler. The tube will say that it is suitable for the edges of sinks, baths, etc. It is not only flexible, but also waterproof;

➤ your finger.

Simply follow the instructions on the tube.

 # Painting

If you are allowed to paint the rooms, go for it. It's not difficult, as long as the walls are not too high. Ceilings are a pain – quite literally, unless you have a neck like a giraffe.

You'll find the instructions on the tin of paint. But which sort of paint?

➤ Emulsion – this is paint for walls and ceilings, not woodwork.

➤ Silk emulsion – emulsion with a shine to it. Looks great and wipes clean, but if your walls have any tiny bumps or dips in them they will show up much more.

➤ Matt emulsion – emulsion which does not have a shine to it. Hard to wipe clean, so gets dirty more quickly, but better for imperfect walls.

➤ Soft-sheen emulsion – a newer type of emulsion, halfway between silk and matt; the best of both worlds. Usually a bit more expensive and may not come in as many colours.

➤ Gloss – for woodwork. Choose one which says 'no undercoat required'; also choose 'non-drip' and 'one-coat'.

➤ Satinwood – also for woodwork. Less shiny than gloss.

Which colour? If you paint a light colour on top of a light colour, your job will be easier and you may not need more than one coat. Light onto dark or dark onto light will certainly mean you'll need at least two coats.

Emulsion paints can be washed off your hands (or anything else) with soap and water, if you do it straight away. Gloss paints will only come off with white spirit or turpentine.

You can paint over wallpaper without problem – though if the paper is embossed (has a raised pattern) this will obviously show through. In that case, you'd be better stripping the wall-paper off first. For this you need a bottle of wallpaper remover/stripper, which you mix with water and slop on, to soak the paper. You then use a wallpaper-stripping knife and a lot of energy and muscle power. If the first piece comes off like a dream, don't celebrate too soon – it's there to lull you into a false sense of confidence. There will be tricky areas and trickier areas and absolutely hellish areas, but you will get there in the end. You may find some small bits of plaster come off with the paper – fill the holes with ready-to-use filler. You may find some enormous pieces of plaster come off – unfortunately, you need a professional plasterer.

➤ Always do the walls before the woodwork.

➤ Use a big brush or roller for walls – and a smaller one for the edges. Use a fairly small brush for woodwork.

➤ Don't put too much gloss on the brush or it will drip –

even if it says non-drip.

➤ Have plenty of ventilation from open windows. Paint fumes, especially gloss, will start by making you feel sick but could also cause breathing problems. Remember – what you breathe in goes into your bloodstream.

➤ Use a DIY mask when painting or using any chemicals; and also when sanding or stripping paint.

➤ Follow the instructions on all paint tins properly.

Mains switches and taps – electricity, water and gas

Electricity

Your electricity mains switch and fuse box will probably be near the front door, perhaps in a hall cupboard. If it's not, go searching. It will be in a cupboard, unless it's in a garage, in which case it will probably be uncovered, on a wall. Wherever it is hiding, you can't miss it – it will have huge thick electric cables going into it, a dial and several switches. One (the largest, usually) will say 'Main switch' on it, or something obviously similar.

How do I switch it off? How do you think? You just switch it in the direction that says 'OFF' and the lights all go out (and things with digital clocks or displays will start flashing and need to be reset).

What about the other switches by the mains switch? (➡️ page 112.) In a newer house, or an old house that has recently been rewired, there will be a separate smaller switch for each different area of the house. This is handy because, if you need to change a fuse somewhere, you can just switch off the relevant part of the house.

> **NOTE:** The wall/ceiling lights will always be on a different circuit from sockets, so make sure you switch off the right one. If in doubt, switch off both the lighting circuit and the sockets circuit. If you're still in doubt, switch off the main mains switch.

Electricity meter

While you are looking at these fascinating switches, take a look at the dial. You'll see a metal disk spinning slowly. No? Do you see a metal disk spinning very quickly? That's because you are using a sickening amount of electricity. Turn something off, or your bill will be sky-high and your impact on the environment will make you feel very guilty indeed.

This is also where you 'read your meter'. Your electricity company will usually send someone to read your meter every three months. If you aren't at home, they will send a bill with an estimate of how much they think you will have used. You can check the real reading by looking at the numbers near your dial. If you have used less than they estimated, you return the bill with the correct figure, and they will send another bill.

Water

More complicated. Back to basics (and believe me, a lot of very clever middle-aged and elderly people don't know about this either).

Water comes into your house or flat through a pipe from the street, under the road. This is called the water main, or mains pipe. It goes straight to your kitchen sink. Always. This means that water from your kitchen sink cold tap is fit to drink, coming fresh from the mains.

There will be two taps (called stopcocks or valves) where you can turn it off completely, stopping any water coming further into your house. You would do this if you had a burst pipe. One will be outside the house, accessed through a small metal plate in your driveway or on the street. Don't worry about this one. The other one is the one you need. It doesn't look exactly like an ordinary tap. It will be circular and it will be directly *on* a pipe somewhere. But where?

The most usual place, at least in a modern house, is under the kitchen sink. Open the cupboard under the sink. If there is a circular tap on the pipe that leads up to the cold tap (or handle, if it's a mixer), it's probably it.

Another possibility is in a downstairs toilet.

It might be behind a removable panel just inside your front door. This is likely in an older house. It might actually be sticking out through a hole in this panel, so that you can turn it without opening any door or panel at all. Look for any odd-looking taps anywhere near your front door (inside).

Finally, it could be in a cellar or under-stair cupboard.

When you find what you think is the mains tap, try it: turn it fully in a clockwise direction; then go to your kitchen and run the cold tap. If it stops after a few seconds (or longer if you live in a flat far away from the entrance to the building), it is the mains stop-valve.

Easy – now you know how to turn the mains off.

✳ TIP: If it is very stiff, use some WD40 spray oil to loosen it. You do not want to wait for an emergency to discover you can't turn it off.

There may *also* be separate shut-off valves for different sections of the plumbing. These will usually look similar to the main stop-valve, but be found either next to the storage tank in the loft or the hot water tank (perhaps in the airing-cupboard). It's a good idea to discover what each does and to label it. But don't worry if it seems complicated – as long as you've found the main one, you're OK.

If you have a water emergency, such as a burst pipe, you will also need to know about two other valves:

➤ The one that feeds the other cold taps in the house. This is by the cold water storage tank, which is probably in the loft. You will see a pipe coming out of the tank and (usually) a red or orange tap/valve on it. Turning this off (clockwise) will stop water going to the cold taps throughout the house.

➤ the one that deals with hot water. This will be by the hot water tank, probably in an airing-cupboard, or possibly in the loft. Again, it is usually orange or red and you turn it clockwise to turn it off.

A word about water

Apart from the kitchen cold tap, the other water outlets are not usually fed directly from the mains. The water goes from the mains pipe into the cold water storage tank in the loft or roof space. From there it goes to:

➤ every other cold tap in the house, whether bath, basin or shower, and into the toilet cisterns;

➤ the hot water tank;

➤ and from there to every hot tap in the house.

Since water from all these taps has come first from a storage tank, you should not really drink it (though most people do and come to no harm). This is because there *may* occasionally be some harmful bacteria in the stored water.

Water leak

➡ Emergency section on page 322.

A dripping tap

A dripping tap is easy to deal with if you have the tools. But you probably haven't if you've only just left home. I suggest that if you are interested (and it *is* a very useful skill and hugely satisfying, as well as saving you money), you either get your APA to show you what you need or buy a simple DIY book. Searching on the Internet will also quite easily find you the right information.

Airlocks in radiators

If a radiator seems cool at the top and hot at the bottom, it probably has an airlock. You need a radiator key. This should be somewhere in the property – ask your landlord. If not, you can buy them from DIY stores very cheaply. Then you locate the small square hole at one of the top corners of the radiator and insert the key. Hold a cloth or piece of toilet paper underneath. Turn the key slightly, anti-clockwise, and you will hear a hissing sound. After a while, the hissing sound will stop and water will bubble out. Quickly tighten the key again.

Not all radiators have these devices. If yours doesn't, unfortunately, it's time to call a plumber. While your plumber is there, get him to explain all the other things you aren't sure about.

Toilets

Blocked toilets – frankly, don't even go there. If you can't see what's blocking it, and bleach doesn't work, call in the experts.

The constantly flushing toilet – yes, sometimes a toilet develops a mind of its own and forgets that it's only supposed to flush when requested; or it may simply dribble water incontinently and irritatingly, day and night. This is where you need to become intimately acquainted with ballcocks. Actually, lifting the lid off a toilet cistern is a fascinating experience for anyone interested in a mechanism of such beautiful simplicity. You can have endless fun lifting and lowering the ballcock arm and seeing what happens. Well, perhaps not endless, but substantial anyway.

But to return to the point, an overactive toilet flush usually means that the arm of the ballcock has become jammed and is fixed at a lower level than it should be, causing the toilet to imagine it has been asked to flush. Simply lift the arm and wiggle it gently and it will usually understand what is required of it. Try flushing again – what happens when the water has filled up again? Does the ballcock return to its correct level (in which case the toilet stops flushing) or does it return to its previous incorrect level?

If the latter, you need a plumber. It's not a complicated job, but there are too many permutations to explain them here. Meanwhile, while you are waiting for the plumber, you need to wedge the ballcock arm at the correct (or slightly higher level). If you are not ingenious enough to work out how to do this, you will have to stand there holding it, or suffer the constant flushing (and waste of water) until the plumber comes. When the plumber comes, watch him/her, so you can see what to do next time.

Water meter

Most people don't have a water meter and therefore don't pay according to how much they use. However, water meters are becoming more common so you should ask your landlord if you have one. If you do, you will want to try not to use too much water. Apparently, bills do tend to be lower with meters.

Frozen pipes

There are two problems with a frozen pipe:
> You can't get any water from it.
> The pipe may crack. While it is still frozen, you won't notice this, but when the water melts, you definitely will.

If a pipe is frozen (i.e. no water comes out), you should turn off the mains tap and then call a plumber. Do not try to thaw it with a hairdryer or anything else, in case you do it too quickly.

Preventing frozen pipes

Proper insulation goes a long way to preventing freezing, and saves you money too. Are the pipes in your loft or roof-space wrapped in insulation or foam casings? If not, get them done – your landlord should want to do this, as it will prevent expensive leaks. If you own your own property or are responsible for it, get a plumber to do this to all exposed pipes in your property.

> In very cold weather, keep the heating/hot water on a low setting most of the time.

> Pipes in lofts may freeze – in cold weather, leave the loft-hatch open a little at night, so that warm air rises into the loft (obviously, not brilliant for your fuel bills or the environment, so much better to make sure the pipes in the loft are properly insulated instead, but if they're not, this is your best way of avoiding disaster).

> Don't put insulation under the cold water tank in the loft – it stops the warm air rising into the tank.

> When you go away for more than a few days in the winter, leave the heating/hot water on a low setting and on a timer. Alternatively, ask a plumber or APA to show you how to drain the system. Some insurance policies insist that you drain the system – check yours.

Gas

You should never do any repairs to a gas pipe or piece of equipment. If you smell gas, call Transco free on 0800 111 999 – any time of day or night.

For full details of how to handle a gas emergency, including smelling gas, ➡ page 318.

Where is the gas mains valve?

Near your gas meter. This may be inside, near your front door, in a cupboard under the stairs, or perhaps in a box just outside your front door. If it is outside, it will be a plastic-covered box and will be opened with a simple plastic key – your landlord should have given you this key. If not, ask, because you must keep it safe and be able to find it.

Inside this box or next to the meter, there will be an obvious tap or valve for you to turn to stop gas coming through into the gas appliance and pipes in the house.

Pest control

Mice, rats, slugs, wasps or ants. Uninvited guests. You don't want them, but you'll probably have them at some point. Time to stop being squeamish and deal with them.

➤ For **mice** and **rats** you need an expert. Don't try putting poison down yourself. Tell your landlord or the council. In some areas, the council charge a fee; in other areas it is free.

➤ **Slugs** feed mainly at night so you may not see them, but if you see silvery trails on your walls, they have been with you while you slept. Talcum powder or flour make a temporary barrier until you can buy some slug pellets from a supermarket or DIY shop. Read the instructions carefully and keep pellets away from food.

➤ **Ants** are the most common household pest. You can buy effective ant powder from supermarkets, but there's no point in using it if you still have the food they like best lying around. So, the first thing to do is to clean your kitchen (or wherever) very carefully, removing all crumbs from cracks in the walls, surfaces or sinks; keep all sweet foods in closed jars; wash out any empty sweet drink cartons and dispose of all rubbish properly. Put ant powder in places where you have seen ants, particularly near cracks.

➤ **Wasps** and **bees** are definitely cases for an expert. Call the council (who may charge) or a private firm. If you have to pay, there should be a guarantee that if the nest returns to the same place they will treat it free.

Calling in the experts

Sometimes you will need an expert to help you. The problem is, how do you know who is an expert? After all, the expensive cowboys are not exactly going to wear a badge saying, 'I'm an expensive cowboy'. Here are my top tips, though I could do with following them myself sometimes:

➤ Spend some time identifying these wonderful experts *before* you actually need them. Ask neighbours who they would recommend. Phone around and tell your chosen professionals that you have just moved in and you want to know what their call-out charges and hourly rates are.

➤ A 24-hour emergency tradesperson will be more expensive than one with regular hours – but you'll still need those emergency numbers as well.

➤ A call-out charge is an amount which you have to pay before they've started doing anything. Usually, this will also cover the first hour of work – but check.

➤ Keep the numbers by the phone.

➤ Get your water/central heating boiler serviced once a year. Do this in the summer or autumn – don't wait till winter.

➤ If it's not an immediate emergency, get at least three quotes and tell each one that you are getting other quotes. Negotiate. Say you can't really afford that and you are desperate – could they please do it a little more cheaply and you will recommend them to all your friends.

➤ For anything involving gas (i.e. your gas central heating/hot water system) you must use someone who is CORGI-registered. For ordinary plumbers, choose one who is a member of the Institute of Plumbers. The two most common quality assurances for electricians are membership of the NICEIC (National Inspection Council for Electrical Installation Contracting) and SELECT. Electricians' adverts in the phone book will tell you this.

➤ Do not pay any money at all until the job is done.

➤ Once they are in the house, tell them that your father/mother/uncle works for the Trading Standards Office – that should keep them in line.

➤ Ask what guarantee there is for the job – in other words, if the problem recurs in a week, what will they do about it? My plumber says that if anything goes wrong within a month of him coming to the house, he will fix it for free – this is a very good idea, because there have been stories of people coming to fix something but actually tampering with your boiler so that it goes wrong again later. I apologize to all the utterly honest tradespeople out there, but these things must be considered.

➤ If they add VAT to the cost, ask them to give you their VAT number. Tradespeople who are VAT-registered must add VAT of 17.5%. If they are not registered, they can't charge it and you shouldn't pay. They might say that if you pay cash, they won't charge VAT – they are not supposed to do that.

➤ If a plumber/electrician/other professional starts to bamboozle you with words and explanations, and much talk of optical spigots and sealed systems and ratcheted condenser valves, say, 'This all sounds really interesting – could you repeat it so I can write it down and tell my parents exactly what the problem was.' If all the fancy words then start to dry up, be suspicious. Be very suspicious.

➤ If possible, stay with the person and watch what he/she is doing. Tell them you have a huge fascination for the inner workings of combination boilers.

➤ If you think you have been ripped off, your local Trading Standards Office will advise you. If you write a cheque but discover a few hours later that the work was rubbish and the problem isn't fixed, phone the tradesperson back and explain the problem. Say that if he/she cannot come and fix it within twelve hours, you will have to phone your bank and cancel the cheque. You can do this – it is called 'stopping' a cheque, and it means the money will not leave your account. This is why it is better to write a cheque than pay cash.

➤ However you pay, ask for a receipt – and make sure you can read it.

➤ When you find a tradesperson who does a good job at a fair price, use him/her again. If you find one that turns up at the time promised, sing it from the rooftops – that's world-shattering news.

Safety in the home

Security

➤ Make sure all outside doors and windows have locks.

➤ Windows should have catches so that they cannot be pulled open from outside, even when they are not fully closed – if this is not the case, do not sleep with your window open, especially if you live on the ground floor.

➤ Do not have your name or address attached to your keys – just a phone number.

➤ If you think your door lock has been tampered with, call a locksmith and get the lock changed.

➤ After dark, keep some lights on in the house and keep the curtains closed.

➤ If you go away, use a couple of timer-switches so lights can be on at night.

➤ Install a special light fitting which makes a light come on after dark – you can buy one that fits into the existing fitting just like a light bulb.

Going away?

➤ Tell someone you trust.

➤ If possible, ask someone to come in the morning and evening to deal with lights and curtains. This may seem like a big favour to ask, but you can offer to do the same for them.

Fire

Install smoke detectors in as many rooms as possible. They are very cheap to buy and require no complicated installation – some just stick onto the ceiling with sticky pads. Follow the instructions for the best place to have them. They save lives – smoke kills more people than flames, and the smoke comes much earlier than the flames.

Check smoke detector batteries regularly and keep spare batteries – they are usually the little rectangular 9 volt ones

Most fires are caused by smokers. Don't let smokers smoke in their bedrooms.

Candles are also a common cause of fires, especially if you've had a party and drunk too much to notice. Never put them near curtains or on low tables.

Other fires are caused by faulty electrical equipment: do not use equipment with frayed wires, loose plugs or anything that makes you think it is not in perfect condition. Do not leave an oven or washing machine or dishwasher on when you leave the house.

When you leave the house, check that heaters, irons and cooking appliances are all turned off. And candles are blown out...

Leave internal doors shut – it delays the spread of fire.

Do you know what to do if there is a fire? There are a few simple tips that can save your life. ➡ page 316 in the Emergency section.

Carbon monoxide poisoning

On average, there are fifty deaths a year in the UK from carbon monoxide poisoning in the home. If your home is at risk, you will not smell it. It can start to affect you quite slowly and mildly over days or weeks – you may often feel nauseous or have frequent headaches, and find that you feel better when you are out of the house. Or it can happen suddenly while you are asleep one night – and you may not wake up. I don't want to alarm you, but it is something you have to know about. It is a danger that should never harm anyone, because it is very simple to prevent and detect.

Prevent

Only a faulty appliance or gas boiler, or one that is not properly ventilated, will produce carbon monoxide inside the house. Get your landlord to get the appliance serviced – today. Or ask to see the gas safety certificate, which should not be more than a year old and should be signed by a CORGI-registered plumber or heating engineer.

Detect

Buy a carbon monoxide detector from a DIY shop. It is simple and very cheap. The battery-operated ones are best. Put one in every room where there is a gas appliance, including the bathroom if you have one of those water heaters that springs to life when you run a hot tap. Don't forget the kitchen.

Electricity

Electric items should never come in contact with water or steam (obviously kettles, etc. are designed specially, but you still must never put the kettle or the base of it into water). Never take a hairdryer or electric heater into a bathroom (unless the heater is designed for bathrooms and is installed properly).

Don't use any item with a frayed wire/cable or loose plug. Get it repaired or chuck it out.

Never put anything metal into the toaster. Unplug it and tip it upside down. Sorry, I should have warned you that a whole load of disgusting antique toast crumbs would fall out. Very carefully insert a plastic knife or wooden spoon to release your mangled teacake.

Unplug electrical items during a thunder storm, especially computers and TVs. Better still, buy a power-surge preventer for the computer, which will stop damage to it in a storm. Available from anywhere where you buy computers, and most DIY stores.

Unplug electrical items when you leave the house for a long period – but *don't* ever unplug the fridge or freezer.

Gas

Don't mess around with gas. If you can smell it or are worried, ➡ page 318 in the **Emergencies** section.

Danger points in the house

> ➤ Electric items in the bathroom pose a serious risk of electrocution and death.
> ➤ Frayed electric wires or ill-fitting plugs mean you risk fire or electrocution.
> ➤ Leaving a hob-ring on is a fire risk.
> ➤ Carbon monoxide leaking from a gas appliance (➡ page 136).
> ➤ Gas fires/hob-rings are at risk of being accidentally turned on without lighting the gas. Fortunately, gas smells very strong so you will probably smell it within a few seconds.

Chemical-free living

It's not possible to eliminate chemicals entirely from your life and it's also unhealthy and pointless to worry about every breath you take. However, there are some things that we can all do which will help reduce the harmful chemicals that enter our bodies. Here are some tips:

> ➤ When you use a chemical product, use as little as possible.
> ➤ Choose eco-friendly or natural products where you have a choice.
> ➤ Choose organic foods if you can afford them.
> ➤ Buy fruit and veg only when they are in season – fruit and veg out of season will have needed more pesticide and fertilizer to produce them.
> ➤ Get rid of all carpets if possible – they trap dust, chemicals and mould.
> ➤ Open your windows often – but not if you live in a traffic-filled area (if that's the case, invest in a good fan and air filter).
> ➤ Avoid using plastic containers for food; avoid drinking from plastic beakers or wrapping food in plastic bags or clingfilm.
> ➤ Buy a water filter and only drink filtered water.
> ➤ Don't smoke indoors (well, don't smoke at all, actually) and don't allow others to smoke indoors. Particles of smoke will settle and build up in your furnishings, etc.
> ➤ Don't dry clothes inside. The moisture will seep into the walls (unless you have windows open) and create an environment for mould. Mould spores are unhealthy, producing their own toxic chemical.

➤ Store all chemicals outside. Paints, petrol, solvents, etc. should be in a garden shed or garage.

➤ Wash curtains often, or replace with blinds.

➤ Have as few soft furnishings as possible (i.e. curtains, cushions, carpets and rugs). They trap dust and chemicals.

➤ Vacuum your mattress cover – it may contain millions of dust mites and a lot of your skin (and maybe the skin of the previous owner...).

➤ Don't use chipboard. It contains formaldehyde, which is released into the air you breathe.

➤ Buy lots of bicarbonate of soda and try using it for almost any cleaning job, including washing clothes (in a washing machine or by hand), removing stains from pretty much anything, cleaning out glass jars and unblocking sinks.

➤ Don't use commercial air fresheners. Sprinkle bicarbonate of soda on furnishings, or leave an open pot of it in the fridge. It soaks up odours.

➤ Take off your shoes in the house. Our pavements are caked in toxic chemicals and you'll tread them all through your house.

➤ Look at the ingredients in the food that you buy and choose the simplest.

➤ Don't buy salad, such as lettuce, in those handy pre-packed bags. They have often been produced with methods that would make your stomach crawl, may contain residues of many heavy doses of fertilizers and pesticides, may well have been soaked in bleach and produced by badly-paid workers in horrible conditions, in countries where the climate was not designed to produce this sort of product. Buy local lettuce, whole, in season. If it's not lettuce season, don't eat lettuce.

Troubleshoot

➤ To find professional
tradespeople in your area,
the Yellow Pages phone
book or www.yell.com are
your best bet. If you
haven't got a Yellow Pages
phone book, phone 0800
671444 and ask – it's free.

➤ To get advice on how to
remove a particular stain
from anything, visit
www.howtocleananything
.com.

Food matters

Contents

Introduction 145

Essential items for your store cupboard or fridge 146

Essential equipment ... .148
Not essential, but very useful 150

Using electrical items in the kitchen 151
Ovens 151
Fridge 155
Freezer 156
Microwave 159

Food hygiene and safety 162
Personal hygiene 162
Handling food 163
Storing food 164
How long can I leave food out of the fridge safely? 165
How long can I keep leftovers for? 165
What is the correct temperature of my fridge? 165

Special storage tips 166
Heating and cooking 166
Shopping hygiene 168
Cleaning the kitchen 168

Enjoying food 169
Especially for vegetarians .170
Vegan? 172
Other special diets 172
Eating fruit and veg 172
Cheap eating 174

Beginning to cook   176

Troubleshoot 179

Introduction

You may well be one of those frighteningly practical people who has cooked confidently from an early age and who can already rustle up a three-course meal at the same time as writing a 5000 word essay on the impact of the Industrial Revolution. But do you know how to defrost a freezer? Or how long you can keep leftovers for? Or the correct temperature of a fridge? And how to avoid campylobacter poisoning? If not, this section is for you – as well as for all those others whose cooking skills extend as far as using a kettle and toaster and not much further.

And if you think *you* are worried about not knowing a thing about cooking, I can tell you that whoever has been cooking your meals up to now is a lot more worried. This chapter is designed to take everyone's fears out of the kitchen and to fill you with competence and your adult relatives with happy amazement. You too can cook a great meal, and by the end of this chapter you will be able to entertain your own parents or any other sceptical adult. Home cooking is healthier and much cheaper than ready meals or fast food. It's also fun and easy, once you know a few simple things.

Essential items for your store cupboard or fridge

Cupboard

➤ Salt
➤ **Whole black pepper corns** (and pepper-grinder)
➤ **Self-raising flour** (if you want to make cakes)
➤ **Plain flour** (*lots* of uses)
➤ **Sugar** (caster sugar is better for cooking)
➤ **Dijon mustard** (great for flavouring casseroles, etc. even if you don't think you like it)
➤ **Baking powder** (only if you like baking cakes)
➤ **Vinegar** (red wine and cider vinegar if possible, but one of the two will do)
➤ **Olive oil** (virgin is more versatile than extra virgin)
➤ **Sunflower oil** (olive oil is not great for frying eggs or eggy toast, for example)
➤ **Cornflour** (for thickening sauces)
➤ **Stock cubes** (vegetable or chicken)
➤ **Worcestershire sauce** (great for flavouring)
➤ **Paprika** (a red pepper powder, nice and spicy)
➤ **Tins of chopped tomatoes**
➤ **Dried herbs** (especially **thyme** or **mixed herbs**)

Fridge

➤ Tomato purée (refrigerate once opened)
➤ Butter/margarine
➤ Eggs
➤ Milk
➤ Onions (useful for flavouring virtually anything savoury)
➤ Marmalade, jam
➤ Cheese
➤ Fruit juice

For quick meals

Cupboard
➤ Pasta (dried, any shape you like)
➤ Pasta sauces (in jars)
➤ Pilchards/sardines/tuna
➤ Baked beans
➤ Tinned soup
➤ Rice/couscous

Freezer
➤ Oven chips
➤ Peas
➤ Mince (or vegetarian alternative)
➤ Bread, including **garlic bread**
➤ White fish or **fish fingers**

Essential equipment

During editorial conversations about this section, there were differing views on what was 'essential'. Some people revealed fascinating passions for peculiar instruments and we had heated arguments about the relative merits of tongs or spatulas. Wooden spatulas fought plastic ones and bizarre practices involving oven cloths were exposed. To be honest, I just let them get on with it and ignored everything they said. The following list consists of what I personally consider essential. And if you think I've got something wrong, I really don't want to know.

➤ 2 or 3 saucepans, preferably non-stick, including one large and one small;

➤ 2 or 3 ovenproof dishes, including one large and one small, and at least one with a lid. To save money, and washing-up, choose something which looks nice enough to go straight on the table. Plain white or blue is perfect – classic and long-lasting;

➤ Kettle (you *could* use a saucepan, but the water may taste of what you last cooked);

➤ Toaster (you *can* do it under a grill, but you will burn the toast – trust me);

➤ At least one metal baking tray – for cooking oven chips, fish fingers, roast potatoes and vegtables, etc;

➤ Metal roasting tin – for roasting meat/chicken;

➤ 2 wooden spoons;

➤ 2 small sharp knives;

➤ Larger sharp knife or carving knife;

➤ Ladle, or large metal or plastic spoon;

- ➤ Fish slice (yes, a wooden spatula would do);
- ➤ Tin-opener;
- ➤ Corkscrew and bottle-opener;
- ➤ Hand whisk (unless you have an electric one ➥ below. And I don't recommend those ones with a handle you turn – a one-handed one is much better);
- ➤ 2 mixing bowls – one large, one smaller;
- ➤ 1 or 2 litre measuring jug (can double up as another mixing bowl);
- ➤ Large sieve (use it for draining pasta/veg, as well as sifting flour or lumps in sauce);

> **NOTE:** If you just have one sieve, make it a) big and b) fine-meshed.

- ➤ 2 chopping boards (non-wood is easier to clean);
- ➤ Kitchen scissors;
- ➤ 3 or more tea towels for drying dishes;
- ➤ Cloths for wiping sides;
- ➤ Washing-up brush and scourer;
- ➤ Oven cloth for handling hot items;
- ➤ Set of cutlery (enough for at least 4–6 people);
- ➤ Set of plates, bowls, etc. (enough for at least 4–6 people);
- ➤ Mugs;
- ➤ Electric hand mixer – some might say not essential but I disagree. It opens up a whole world of things you can make without breaking your arm. It doesn't need to be expensive, starting at around £15. Useful for cakes, pancakes, dealing with lumpy sauce, lots of puddings and whipping cream. Choose one that has a blender attachment, then you can also blend soups, smoothies or milkshakes.

Not essential, but very useful

➤ Steamer (cheap collapsible one to go inside saucepan) – steamed veg is healthier than boiled, and it's quicker because you don't have to boil a large amount of water;

➤ Wooden breadboard and knife;

➤ Potato masher – a fork works reasonably well instead;

➤ Tongs – for picking up objects like sausages;

➤ Spatula – wooden, for turning things over.

(That should satisfy both the tongs and spatula fans.)

Using electrical items in the kitchen

If the electrical items in your kitchen do not have the instruction manuals with them, ask your landlord or the previous occupants. It is not only safer, it also means you will get the most out of the machines and be able to look after them properly. Tell your landlord that it is dangerous for you not to have the proper instructions in writing and that, if he/she can't get them for you, you cannot be responsible for looking after them properly – that should do the trick. If your landlord can't provide them, contact the manufacturers yourself: go to an electrical store and either ask them for the manuals or ask for the manufacturers' helplines and ask them to send them to you. This should be free.

Below are some general but very useful and important points about common equipment.

Ovens

Hob
Strictly speaking, the hob is not the oven. The hob is the bit you put pans on, while the oven is the part you open up. If your oven is built into the kitchen sides, the hob may be immediately above the oven, or not.

Single oven
This is an oven with one compartment. There will usually be a grill at the top, which you *usually* can't use at the same time as the oven (➡ **Oven tips**, below).

Double oven

This has two compartments, a smaller one above a larger one. The grill will be in the upper section and the upper section can be used as an oven instead (not *usually* at the same time as the grill, but at the same time as the lower section). Handy because you can either:

a) grill in the upper section at the same time as cooking something in the lower compartment or

b) cook different things at different temperatures, using both compartments.

Fan oven

A fan oven cooks food faster than a conventional oven and it reaches its desired temperature very quickly. It may be single or double, but the fan will usually only be in the larger section. If you have a fan oven, you need to reduce the times and temperatures given in recipes by about 10–15%. (If you have a fan oven, it will have a little icon something like this 🌀 probably by the control knob.)

Gas or electric?

A very common combination is a gas hob and an electric oven. For the *hob* (➡ **Hob tips** page 153), gas is instant and very easily controlled, so you don't have to wait for a ring to get cooler or hotter while you are cooking. But lighting a gas *oven* can be tricky (and sometimes moderately frightening), so many people prefer electric.

Oven tips

➤ Check the instructions that came with your oven, to see whether you are allowed to have the oven door closed while the grill is on. Many grills do not have thermostats to tell when they are too hot and you seriously risk a fire.

➤ If yours is a gas oven, do not attempt to light it without the written instructions – some have an automatic starter button, but older models may need to be lit with a match or special lighter (tricky and frankly unpleasant, not to mention dangerous, in my opinion).

➤ Make sure that any item you put in an oven is 'ovenproof'. It's fine to put table plates/bowls in for a very few minutes to warm them, but don't let them get too hot. Never put glass in the oven. However, there is a material called Pyrex, which looks like glass but is designed to go in the oven.

➤ A non-fan oven will take at least five minutes to reach its temperature. Turn it on before you need it.

➤ Recipes usually give temperatures for °C/°F/gas. Which is your oven?

➤ If you put lots of things in an oven at the same time, the food will take longer to cook.

➤ Don't open the door while you are baking a cake. It will sink.

➤ Each time you open the door, you lower the temperature considerably.

➤ It is useful to have an oven thermometer – it's the only way to know whether your oven is reaching the temperature you intend. They cost very little.

Hob tips

➤ Never put glass or china/pottery on the hob, even briefly. The rule for hobs is *metal only* (unless an item specifically says it can go directly on a hob/cooker). If your hob is something fancy like halogen, refer to the manufacturer's booklet to see what you can use. If in doubt, go to an electrical/gas appliance shop and ask for advice.

➤ With gas, the flames should not go up the side of the pan – turn the flame down accordingly.

➤ Always have the saucepan handles facing to the side, away from other rings. If the handles face towards you, you risk knocking the whole pan over – and it's also very dangerous if a child is around.

➤ Once something comes to the boil, reduce the heat till it is only just boiling ('simmering'), to avoid burning and to reduce power usage.

➤ Do not use metal spoons in non-stick saucepans; don't scrub them with harsh scourers either. With stuck-on food, leave them to soak in warm water.

➤ Do not let food boil dry – add more water to potatoes, rice or pasta, for example.

➤ Wipe up spillages as soon as the hob is cool enough to touch. If you wait a week, it will have dried to a disgusting gooey charcoal and you will not enjoy cleaning it. It will also attract flies and bacteria.

Cleaning tips

➤ Don't let your oven or hob become too engrimed with burnt-on food. Clean it every now and then. Allow to cool first, then switch the oven light on, but not the heat (do this by *starting* to turn the oven on, but stopping before you hear the heat start up); use a thick paste made with bicarbonate of soda and scrub the enamel (shiny) parts with a scourer.

➤ Some ovens are called 'self-cleaning'. The self-cleaning parts have a sort of rough texture and you obviously don't need to clean them. I don't know why – I think it's magic and it makes me wonder why everything can't be self-cleaning.

➤ Use Spotless or a similar biodegradable paste (➡ pages 94–5).

➤ There are very powerful oven cleaners – they do work, but they are very dangerous if not treated with respect, and I still have a small mark on my nose to prove it.

➤ Always let pans cool before putting water on them.

For a pan fire, ➡ the section on **Fire** page 316.

Fridge

OK, so it's a bit obvious how to use a fridge, isn't it? You'd be surprised.

The bottom of a fridge is the coldest part. Goodness knows why they always put salad boxes there, since salad doesn't like to be very cold. Keep salad at the top and raw meat, fish and poultry at the bottom.

The correct temperature for a fridge is between 0°C and 5°C. A cheap fridge thermometer will tell you if yours is right. Don't keep opening the door – you'll instantly lose the correct chill factor. If your fridge is warmer than 5°C you risk the food going off and making you ill. And even 5°C is only suitable for things like salad and veg. Meat, fish, paté, etc. will need to be stored at a maximum of 3–4°C.

Always wrap things in clingfilm or put them in covered containers. Strong smells will affect milder things. (However, some plastics may contaminate food with their chemicals, so use plastic sparingly and don't use it for hot food.)

Raw meat or fish should *never* be allowed to touch or drip onto anything else. Ideally, keep raw meat in the bottom compartment, well wrapped up.

Clean any spillage and regularly clean the fridge with a mild detergent or very diluted bleach solution or solution of bicarbonate of soda (➥ pages 102–3). Every 2–3 weeks should be fine, though you won't find many people who do it that often. Do do it if you've spilt something, though.

Check labels to see if food should be refrigerated after opening and then used within a certain time.

Inside the fridge, at the back, you'll find a small hole and a ridge which collects condensation and drains it away. Occasionally this becomes blocked and starts to overflow. Gently clean it, poking carefully with something like a teaspoon wrapped in kitchen paper. Use a mild bleach solution to clean it.

A fridge needs some space behind it as it gets hot at the back. Don't allow this space to be blocked or covered. Pull it

4

FOOD MATTERS

out a few centimetres from the wall. The manufacturer's handbook will tell you the ideal distance.

To deal with smells in a fridge, leave a small dish of bicarbonate of soda open on one of the shelves.

Freezer

Though you can live without a freezer, they are very useful and they tend not to be expensive. Old-fashioned fridges sometimes have a freezer compartment inside the fridge – these are not usually very satisfactory: they are tiny, often not cold enough and tend to clog up with ice. However, you may well have a fridge with a separate freezer compartment – a 'fridge-freezer': this will be very useful indeed.

Isn't frozen food unhealthy? Don't all the nutrients disappear?

No. Freezing prevents the degeneration of food. Most bacteria can't grow (though most don't die either) and most nutrients are not destroyed. Frozen veg is usually frozen very soon after harvesting, so there is no time for loss of nutrients: this means that frozen veg may have more goodness than supermarket veg that has sat around for days.

Does frozen food keep for ever?

No. It tends to dry out and lose texture after a while. When you buy frozen food or food that has freezing instructions, it will say how long you can freeze it for. If you freeze it for a while longer, you will not come to harm but the food may have passed its best and be less tasty.

Defrosting a freezer

If ice builds up in the freezer, you will need to defrost it. If you don't, ice will stop the door shutting properly. Then the food will thaw and you will lose it (because you can't freeze it twice

➡ **Freezer tips** below). You should only have to do this about once a year – if your freezer needs it more often, it may not be cold enough. Turn it down. **To defrost a freezer:**

➤ Remove the food and wrap it in newspaper, leaving it in the coldest place you can. Do not let anything thaw – ice cream thaws very quickly so put it in the fridge and surround it with other frozen items.

➤ Switch the freezer off at the plug and leave the door open.

➤ Put newspapers on the floor, and shallow containers to catch the drips (a tray works well).

➤ Wait for the ice to melt. Speed this up by putting a bowl of very hot water in the freezer. Replace it when the water no longer steams. After a while, you will be able to lift off large pieces of ice. The whole process may take a couple of hours, depending how much ice there is. Do *not* be tempted to use a knife to scrape more ice off – you could damage the freezer or a wire. I speak from experience.

➤ When all the ice has gone, clean the inside with a weak bleach or detergent solution.

➤ Switch the freezer back on and shut the door. Wait till it is cold before replacing the food.

Freezer tips

➤ The coldest part of a freezer should be -18°C or colder.

➤ When food has thawed or begun to thaw, don't freeze it again – unless you cook it first. For example, you could take raw mince out, cook it and then freeze it, but not ice cream because you are not going to cook it.

➤ When you take food from the freezer, it should be refrigerated and eaten within 24–36 hours.

➤ Some food should be cooked from frozen (like peas and chips); others must be thawed first. Check the instructions on the packet.

➤ Some freezers have a 'quick-freeze' section at the top – if yours does, put items in here first to freeze them quickly.

➤ Don't over-fill your freezer – it won't be so effective and the door might not shut properly, causing you to lose everything.

➤ Ideally, you should thaw something by leaving it in the fridge, not at room temperature. If you want it thawed quickly because you want to use it immediately, either sit it in a bowl of warm water or use the microwave – but you must use it immediately, because either of these methods quickly raises the outer parts of the food to a temperature where germs breed.

➤ Wrap raw meat, fish and poultry in plastic bags, making sure the outside is not contaminated. Store away from foods like ice cream which will be eaten without cooking.

> **!** **WARNING:** Do not freeze things in glass bottles. If freezing in a plastic bottle, do not fill the bottle too full and do leave the lid off or loose while freezing – the liquid will expand. The voice of bitter experience again...

Suitable freezer containers are: plastic containers – freeze with lid off, then put lid on once frozen; freezer-proof containers which may also be oven-proof; and plastic bags. But note the comments about the use of plastic: ➡ page 155. If you use plastic, make sure it is for food use, and don't put the food in while it's hot.

What can I freeze?

Most food will say on the packet whether you can freeze it or not. What if it doesn't? As a general rule, if it doesn't say 'may be frozen' and if it's something you won't cook before eating, don't freeze it – for example, bought paté, ham, bought ready-cooked meat. This is because it *may* have been frozen by the manufacturers already. Some things wouldn't harm you, they would just lose their texture when frozen, but other things may harm you, so don't freeze something if it doesn't say you can. If it says it may be frozen, of course it may be. And if it's something you made yourself, such as paté, you can also freeze it because you know it hasn't already been frozen.

YES
- Bread
- Soups
- Stews
- Mince
- Pies
- Cooked pasta
- Raw/cooked meat/fish

NO
- **Fruit/veg** unless expertly frozen
- **Cream** – unless whipped
- **Yogurt**
- **Jelly**
- **Eggs**

> **(!) WARNING:** Always freeze things when they are as fresh as possible. Freezing does *not* kill most bacteria – it simply stops them multiplying further. Only cooking at a high temperature kills bacteria.

> **(!) WARNING:** If there's a power cut or your freezer breaks down, do not open the door. The food will stay frozen for up to 24 hours if the door has not been opened. Even opening it once dramatically reduces this time.

Microwave

Very useful indeed, especially for one or two people (because it's best for small quantities). You can defrost or cook most foods very quickly indeed. They come in a range of prices, starting at about £40. You can also get more expensive ones called 'combination'. These also enable you to use them like a normal oven or grill – useful if you don't have much space or your oven is very small.

A microwave oven heats food by sending out short waves (micro-waves) which shake the water molecules in the food, producing heat. This is why, if you put in something with absolutely no water molecules, such as a dry plate, no heat is produced (unless there's already some condensation in the oven). It's also why something with lots of water (such as a cup of coffee or milk) will take longer to heat than something with less water content, such as a piece of bread.

Microwave tips

➤ How powerful is your microwave? You need to know what wattage it is: whether it is, for example, a 650W or 800W or whatever. The higher the wattage, the quicker the food will cook. Microwave food instructions will give different cooking times for different powers of oven. The wattage should be printed on the outside of the oven – you will find a symbol like this:

➤ You can use almost any utensil in a microwave, *except* metal, tin foil or fine glass/crystal (only because the heat from the food will shatter the glass). Make sure there is no metal at all in the utensil – sparks will fly if there is. Thick glass is fine for warming liquid but not for making it very hot. You may have bowls made of Pyrex – these are toughened glass and are perfect for microwaving. They can also go in a normal oven.

➤ Although the utensil will not be heated directly by the microwaves, once the food is hot the container will take on heat as well, so you should still use an oven glove.

➤ Food should always be covered, but with space for the steam to escape. If it's not covered, it will a) dry out and b) explode very messily. Trust me.

- If one potato takes three minutes to bake, two potatoes will take six minutes.
- Microwaves do not actually penetrate more than a few centimetres into the food. This means that you need to stir things regularly to ensure that they heat evenly. For something that can't be stirred (like a baked potato), you need to allow time for the heat to transfer gradually throughout the item. This is why microwave ovens are best for smaller items – larger ones *will* cook, but will take much longer.
- Sugar and fat reach a higher temperature than water. Be very careful when eating such foods from a microwave – there may be incredibly hot spots inside them.
- If you don't know how long to cook something for, try one minute at a time and see what happens. You will soon get to know how long something takes.
- Always allow a 'standing time' of at least a minute at the end of cooking – this is to let the heat spread evenly throughout the food.
- Microwaved food tends to be pale-looking – if you want something to have a nice crispy golden outside, finish it off in the oven (e.g. a baked potato).

WARNING: Never, ever, ever put an egg in a microwave. It will explode. It may do this just after you've opened the door, which is highly dangerous, not to mention extremely messy. Have you ever tried to clean a kitchen ceiling while calling an ambulance? I know someone this happened to – she was lucky not to lose the sight in one eye.

WARNING: Check regularly to make sure there is no damage to the door seal. If there is, stop using it and get it checked by an electrician.

Food hygiene and safety

Food poisoning is unpleasant at the very least. Occasionally, it can land you in hospital. Very occasionally, it can even kill. Each year in the UK, it is estimated that around 5.5 million people become ill from the food they eat. That's one in ten.

Most food poisoning is caused by poor hygiene or food safety in the home, not in a restaurant. Most of it is also extremely easy to prevent because the three main risks are very easily avoided. These risks are:

➤ inadequate cooking/heating;

➤ inadequate storage/refrigeration;

➤ raw or contaminated food touching ready-to-eat food – including being transferred by your hands onto a work surface, knife or plate.

Here are the best ways to reduce your risk of food poisoning.

Personal hygiene

Your hands carry germs from one activity to the other. You have bacteria on your hands pretty much all the time – and most of the time you won't get ill. But there are certain activities which will multiply the nasty bugs on your hands and you should be very careful to wash your hands after *all of them*, and especially before you prepare or eat food for yourself or anyone else.

➤ Going to the toilet – around half of all men and a quarter of all women do not wash their hands after going to the toilet;

➤ Handling raw meat/fish/poultry;

➤ Changing a baby's nappy;

➤ Caring for an ill person;

➤ Coughing or sneezing;

➤ Picking your nose – no, of course *you* don't do that;

➤ Handling pets or cleaning a cat's litter tray;

➤ Gardening.

Rinsing your hands under a cold tap does not count. You need hot water and soap. Remember your fingernails and rings. As many germs could be lurking under your ring as there are people in Europe. Take it off. Dry hands on a clean towel or kitchen paper. A thousand times more germs are spread by damp/wet hands than by dry hands.

> **!** **WARNING:** Another favourite place for lurking bugs is a damp towel or tea towel in a lovely warm kitchen. Dry all towels and tea towels after use and wash regularly. And the worst place of all is the cloth you use for wiping kitchen sides.

Handling food

➤ Wash your hands before handling any food and after touching raw meat, fish or poultry.

➤ Everything that raw meat, fish or poultry touches could be contaminated by harmful bacteria – so clean up as you go: remember taps, knives, plates, bowls, chopping-boards and anything which the food or your hands touched.

➤ Keep raw meat, fish and poultry away from other foods. In the fridge, they should be wrapped and stored at the bottom; on your work surface, they should be well away from other foods (to avoid accidental splashing) and should never share utensils.

➤ Don't just wipe your hands on a cloth – the bacteria are now on the cloth.

➤ Don't prepare food directly on the kitchen side or table – use a chopping-board or plate.

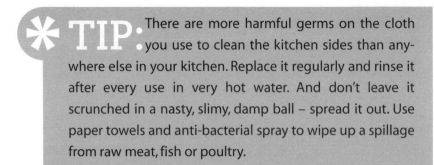

Storing food

Check the storage instructions on the food. No food lasts forever.

> ➤ **Sell-by date:** a shop must not sell food after this date. It may, however, be safe to *eat* after this date. There should also be a 'use-by' or 'eat-by' date.

> ➤ **Use-by/Eat-by:** you should not eat it after this date. Some items, such as bread or fruit/veg, will do you no harm, as long as they seem fresh. Others, such as paté or other meat, fish and poultry, should be thrown away.

> ➤ **Best before:** tins, packets and jars usually say 'Best before'. This means that they will do you no harm if you eat them after this date, but they may not be at their best.

Refrigerated food may have further instructions, such as 'Eat within two days of opening'. If you open it actually *on* the 'use-by' date, you should not keep it beyond that date, so you will have to use it that day. People often do eat something that has passed its use-by date, as long as it smells and tastes fine, and most of these people will come to no harm. But I have to be boringly responsible in this book, so my advice is not to do it. And certainly *never* do it with shellfish, paté or anything which you suspect has been out of the fridge for a while during the course of its storage.

Whatever the storage instructions, humans were designed with noses, taste buds and eyes partly in order to tell if food was good to eat – use yours. So, if it smells, tastes or looks wrong, don't eat it – even if it is within its dates.

WARNING: Be careful when shopping. If a packet or tin is damaged, air may have got in. Don't buy it. If you discover it when you get home, take it back next time you go and get a refund or replacement. It should not matter if you've lost your receipt.

If you leave food out uncovered, you will soon be a fly's best friend. And the flies will tell all their fly friends and possibly even have fly babies in your kitchen. Flies have an unattractive habit of sitting on dog shit, cat shit and anything else that you wouldn't want brought in from the street or garden. So, don't leave food uncovered, especially in summer – and wash fruit before you eat it. You never know what's licked it before you.

How long can I leave food out of the fridge safely?

If food should be refrigerated, it can stay out for around two hours once it has reached room temperature, though in very warm conditions you should reduce this. If in doubt, throw it out. And remember about those flies...

How long can I keep leftovers for?

Put them in the fridge straight away (once quickly cooled) and eat them within two days. Or freeze immediately if suitable: for example, stews, mince, casseroles and soups that have not already been frozen.

What is the correct temperature of my fridge?

Colder than 5°C. The coldest part of the fridge (the bottom) should be around 3°C – use this area for meat, fish and rice and the top for things like cheese and salads.

Special storage tips

➤ **Potatoes:** store in a cool place (not the fridge) in a paper or cloth bag to keep the light off them. Don't use a plastic bag – potatoes like to breathe.

> ! **POTATO WARNING:** Potatoes that have started to go green are producing a toxic chemical. If a potato has a small green area, cut it off – the rest of the potato will be fine. If it is largely green, discard it.

➤ **Bananas and avocadoes:** don't put them in the fridge at all unless you actually like them black.

➤ **Jam, marmalade, honey, chocolate spread**, etc: these will last longer if you refrigerate them after opening.

➤ **Eggs:** should be kept in the fridge, but if you are going to boil them, take them out and warm them under running water first – that's the *only* way to stop them cracking. Ignore any old wives who tell you differently.

➤ **Fruit** (apart from bananas): does not need to be kept in the fridge, but it will last longer if it is.

Heating and cooking

Cooking is the only way to kill harmful bacteria. There are some simple rules to follow:

➤ Follow instructions on packets and recipes, but don't trust the times given because your oven might not be the right temperature. Always check that food is piping hot right through. How? By sticking a metal skewer or knife into the thickest part and then holding it against the inside of your wrist. Do the same in several parts of the food.

➤ These meats must *always* be cooked right through, with no pink bits left and no pink juices: chicken, burgers, sausages, minced beef, minced lamb and kebabs.

➤ Joints or steaks of lamb and beef *may* be eaten slightly

pink in the middle – but *not* when minced (because the bacteria in these meats tend to stay on the surface); all the outside parts of the meat must be properly cooked.

➤ Rice can cause a particularly nasty and dangerous type of food poisoning if it is not properly treated after cooking – if it is to be eaten cold, it must be cooled very quickly and kept very well-chilled until needed; it should be re-heated only with great care: frying cooked rice is the best way to ensure that every grain reaches a hot enough temperature to kill the bugs. If in doubt, throw it out. Avoid rice in buffets where you do not entirely trust the hygiene standards. Especially in the summer.

➤ Eggs – there is a small risk of food poisoning from raw or lightly cooked eggs. Government advice is that these people should avoid them: pregnant women, the elderly, young children and babies, and ill people. An egg is cooked properly when the yellow part is completely firm, not soft. For everyone else, a raw or uncooked egg should do no harm, though do make sure they are fresh, using this easy method: fill a deep bowl with cold water. Place the egg in it. The freshest eggs will lie down flat. Less fresh eggs try to stand on end. If an egg tries to swim, bin it: you do not want to smell it – trust me.

Reheating

If you are reheating food that you have already cooked and cooled, be careful of two things:

➤ Make sure you reheat it till it is piping hot all through.

➤ Only do it once.

Cooling

A few important points about cooling:

➤ Don't put hot food in the fridge (or freezer) because you'll raise the temperature for everything else.

➤ Cool it quickly in the coolest place you can find and then refrigerate it. One way to cool food before refrigerating is to place the dish in a bowl of cold water and replace the cold water regularly, till the food is cool.

➤ If you are trying to cool and chill a large amount of food, divide it into smaller portions so it cools more quickly and you can therefore get it in the fridge more quickly.

➤ Your aim is for the food to reach chilling temperature (maximum 5°C) as quickly as possible, without raising the temperature of the fridge.

Shopping hygiene

No, this is not about wearing a mask while out shopping. Nor does it involve taking an anti-bacterial spray and spraying all the other shoppers. There are a few important points about getting your food home safely, though:

➤ Buy cold and frozen foods last so they don't get warm in your trolley.

➤ Keep raw meat, fish and poultry away from other things. The plastic wrapping may leak – put these items in plastic bags to be sure.

➤ If you can't get the food home very quickly, consider using a coolbag for chilled items.

➤ If you have milk delivered (lucky you – most people don't), provide a covered container for the milkman to put the milk in. If you don't, birds may peck the bottles and birds are horrible germy creatures. I don't mean to be anti-bird – of course they are also a beautiful and essential part of the natural world – but they do carry very nasty bacteria in their beaks.

Cleaning the kitchen

➥ Cleaning, pages 101–7

Enjoying food

Now that all the horrible stuff is out of the way, let's look at what we should really be doing with food, which is enjoying it and letting it nourish us. Food is about survival, health and pleasure, and now that you are on your own it's your responsibility. Daunting maybe, but at least now you are in control and that's got to be good. It's what you've been fighting for for the last five years.

Dieticians nowadays don't like to talk about 'bad' food or 'good' food. It's all about balance. Nothing wrong with chips sometimes. Or even a fast-food burger, instant noodles, bar of chocolate or cream cake. Nothing wrong with an occasional ready meal, TV dinner, microwave meal or takeaway.

But if you rely on these things too much, several things will happen. You will probably:

➤ put on weight, which you probably don't want;
➤ not get all the vitamins, etc. that you need;
➤ be ill, because your immune system will be weak;
➤ be poor, because these things end up being expensive;
➤ miss out on the pleasures of being able to cook for yourself;
➤ lose control of what goes into your body – ready meals are of full of hidden ingredients.

Make sure that your weekly diet includes good amounts of all of these things:

➤ Protein: from meat, eggs, fish, dairy products (e.g. cheese and milk), beans and pulses (e.g. peas).
➤ Carbohydrates: from a range of foods such as pasta, rice, potatoes and bread.

- ➤ Fibre: from cereals, fruit and veg, pure fruit juice, beans etc. and wholemeal bread.
- ➤ Vitamins and minerals: from a wide variety of fruits and vegtables – the wider the range you eat, the greater the chance of getting everything you need.
- ➤ Iron: an especially important mineral found mostly in egg yolk, red meat, fortified cereal (check the packet), bread (small amounts), dark green leafy veg (especially spinach) and liver.
- ➤ Calcium: another mineral worth a special mention. It's the one that keeps your bones and teeth strong. It's found mainly in milk, other dairy products (e.g. yogurt), fortified cereal (check the packet) and bread.
- ➤ Fats and oils: fats which are 'unsaturated' are the better ones, found mainly in vegetable oils and olive oil. 'Saturated' fats should be eaten in much smaller quantities, and are found in meats and dairy produce. Fish oils are also very important. These are found in oily fish such as sardines, pilchards, tuna, salmon, herring and mackerel.

If you eat a varied diet, you probably get most of what you need without thinking about it. If you tend to eat the same foods every day, you probably don't. If you eat only pre-cooked meals or convenience foods, you almost certainly don't and you certainly eat too much salt, sugar and fat. Ready meals are incredibly high in these things.

Especially for vegetarians

It is perfectly possible to have a nutritionally excellent diet when you are a vegetarian. In fact, there's evidence to support the view that meat-eaters could be better eating less meat and more of the pulse and cereal-based diet of a vegetarian – and certainly, as far as the environment is concerned, meat-eaters use up more of the world's agricultural land and resources because we have to grow food for the animals before we get the nutrition from it.

However, being a vegetarian does require some extra care. Meat does contain important nutrients – especially protein, iron and other minerals, and B vitamins. Fish also provides vitamins A, D and E and the important mineral iodine. If you make sure that your vegetarian diet contains extra amounts of the following products, you will be fine:

➤ Eggs
➤ Beans, lentils, nuts and pulses
➤ Seeds (e.g. sunflower, sesame) – choose wholegrain bread with seeds
➤ Soya products
➤ Wholemeal bread and wholemeal pasta
➤ Cereal – especially fortified cereals (fortified with vitamins and minerals)
➤ Dairy products – milk, yogurt and cheese
➤ Dark green leafy vegetables
➤ Fruit containing vitamin C (e.g. oranges) – helps our bodies absorb iron

Sunlight is also important because it helps our bodies produce vitamin D, which is not found in plants.

The one nutrient that vegetarians may find hard to consume is B12. It is really only found in animal products – fine if you eat sufficient eggs and dairy produce. B12 is also added to yeast extract (e.g. marmite), fortified cereals, veggie-burgers, soya products and many products designed for vegetarians.

The Vegetarian Society has a great website at www.vegsoc.org.

Do get a good vegetarian cookbook. Most of them include nutritional advice.

Vegan?

If you are a vegan, it is obviously harder to get all the nutrients you need – though all this requires is knowledge and effort. For the best possible advice to keep yourself well and healthy, contact The Vegan Society, or visit their excellent website at www.vegansociety.com. They produce fact sheets and guides to healthy living and eating.

Other special diets

If you have a different dietary requirement, such as gluten-free or wheat-free, the chances are that you will already know very well how to deal with this. Now that you are looking after yourself, however, it definitely makes sense to ensure that you *do* know everything you need to know. Also, new products and ideas are always coming along. The best way to keep ahead of things is to make sure you are in touch with the organization which deals with your particular diet or condition. Ask your GP or health centre about this if you do not already know it.

Eating fruit and veg

Fruit and veg are getting their own special section. We all know we're supposed to eat at least five portions a day. Yet sometimes it just sits there in the bowl, looking pretty and theoretically tempting for a few days, until it starts to wrinkle, fester and collapse and gets thrown away. I think it's because we're all so lazy: by the time we've summoned the effort to walk over to the bowl, pick up an apple, walk over to the sink and wash the apple, we're completely exhausted. And as for the idea of actually peeling an orange – please! All that pith under the thumb nail. So much easier to eat a biscuit.

Pathetic, really.

And then there's the well-known fact that all veg is disgusting. Wrong. Oh, how very wrong you are. So, there are vegetables you don't like? You don't have to eat *those* ones any more. Remember, there is now no nagging adult telling you to eat the greens that he or she chose to serve up to you with a grumpy, 'Like it or leave it' comment. *You* choose the fruit and veg now, and with the skills you are about to learn, it will be a breeze. It will even be a pleasure.

Here are some sneaky ways of getting yourself to eat your famous five portions without even noticing that you've done it:

➤ Drink a small glass of fresh fruit juice. This must be described as 'pure' fruit juice, not 'fruit drink'. 'Made from concentrate' is fine. 'Diluted from concentrate' is not. That's one portion.

➤ Make or buy vegetable soup. A large bowl could be two portions.

➤ Make a banana smoothie or milkshake (you need an electric blender attachment ➡ page 149). That's one more portion. Add about eight strawberries to it and you've got two portions.

➤ Add spinach leaves at the last minute of cooking a stew, casserole, mince dish or pasta sauce – they disappear to virtually nothing and you won't even know they're there. A handful of leaves is another portion.

➤ Make a stir-fry. Even people who claim not to like veg will usually like a stir-fry. You can have lots of meat in it and the veg takes on a completely different taste. (➡ **Stir-fry** on page 178.)

➤ Don't only think apples and bananas. Spare a thought for grapes, plums, kiwis, mangos, lychees and pineapples. And what about tinned fruit? Treat yourself to some strawberries in the summer.

➤ Make use of local farmers' markets. Many towns have daily or weekly markets. Here you will buy food that is cheaper, fresher, healthy and in season. You will be helping yourself and local people and the environment. Time to reward yourself with a mango smoothie, I'd say.

FOOD MATTERS

Cheap eating

Healthy eating does not have to be more expensive than unhealthy eating. Our food in the UK has never been cheaper and supermarkets are driving prices down – very bad news for producers and farmers (and probably the environment), but good news for the home leaver on a budget.

Tips for eating cheaply

➤ Don't buy brand names – choose the shop's own brand. In most cases you can save large amounts of money and notice no difference in taste. Why be ripped off just for the sake of a name? If it really matters to you (hopeless victim of advertising that you are), buy the expensive brand once, then buy the cheaper one next time and transfer it to the expensive-looking container... Or go shopping in disguise and never invite anyone into your kitchen. Or get a life.

➤ A larger packet usually works out cheaper than two smaller ones, so try to buy in bulk. Consider sharing with a friend.

➤ Most supermarkets have a label on the shelf which will say (in very small print) the cost per 100 ml (or whatever). This makes it easy to compare the price of different brands and different sizes.

➤ Look out for special offers – obviously – but don't be tempted to buy something you don't want just because it's cheap.

➤ Make a double quantity and freeze half – this will usually work out cheaper.

➤ Frozen food is often cheaper than fresh, and the quality and nutrition is usually just as good. Frozen peas, chicken, fish and fruit are all great stand-bys.

WARNING: Buying cheap is not always a good idea, however. For example, cheap fish fingers or mince may have much more water or fat and much less fish or meat. Cheap sausages are highly likely to be full of disgusting body parts that you wouldn't even want to feed to your dog. Cheap burgers are likely to have less meat and more fat/water/rubbish. And cheap meat pies are another no-no. Cheap chicken is very likely to be from a chicken that's had a life most people would cringe to think about.

Shopped by Joanna Blythman is the book to read if you want to be rudely woken up to what your supermarket is trying to do to you. You may never dare eat a ready-made meal or bag of supermarket salad again. Put it this way – I read three pages and went straight out to create a vegetable patch. I'm not joking.

Beginning to cook

I thought about including some basic recipes at this point, but there are lots of great cookbooks out there which already do it. Easily my favourite, and the only one I'm going to recommend, is *The Student Cookbook*, published by Hamlyn. It is stylish and beautiful and contains over 200 great, practical, clear recipes, as well as cheap and clever kitchen tips. Why it's called *The Student Cookbook* beats me, though – it's really for any young person setting out for the first time into the wonderful world of cooking.

But one of the best ways to learn to cook is simply to cook, to get out there and do it. So all I'm going to do is arm you with some relatively random but essential bits of knowledge and send you off with your spatula or tongs into the wide and wonderful world of the kitchen.

Beat/whisk

To mix air into something, using a hand whisk or electric mixer (or, if you really want to suffer, a fork). If you are right-handed, use your left hand to tip the bowl slightly, while you use your right hand in a shallow winding motion (as though you were very quickly turning a handle), making the whisk go round and round in the liquid. Do this until the contents of the bowl are as described in the recipe, or simply well blended if it doesn't specify.

Brown

Usually, if a recipe calls for onions, meat or mushrooms, you start by 'browning' them. This means heating some oil in a saucepan or frying pan and frying them over a medium heat, stirring until they begin to be slightly brown. The onions will go transparent and the meat will turn brown on all sides. This adds flavour and seals the juice into the meat.

Cooking methods

- ➤ **Bake:** to cook in an oven with little or no liquid.
- ➤ **Roast:** to cook in an oven with a coating of fat or oil.
- ➤ **Fry:** to heat with oil in a frying-pan until brown.
- ➤ **Steam:** to cook over boiling water.
- ➤ **Boil:** to cook in boiling water. Put in a pan on a hot ring until the liquid is bubbling vigorously. Usually, you then reduce the heat till you have a 'simmer'.

Liquid

If you cook something without enough liquid, it will go dry and may burn at the bottom. Some things don't need liquid (like a roast joint). If something in a pan seems to be getting too dry, add more of whatever liquid was originally used – for example, milk, water, tomato juice, stock or cider.

Salt

Without it many foods, such as veg or sauces, taste bland. Add it a little at a time, tasting as you go. If you put too much salt in, it will taste awful. If that happens, you can try diluting the dish by adding milk, cream or crème fraiche (if suitable for the thing you are making). Or if you can't do that, you can try putting a couple of large potatoes in and cooking further – it's supposed to draw the salt out and you then throw the potatoes away. I've never tried it, because of course I've never put too much salt in...

Simmer

When you have got something to boil, reduce the heat to the lowest possible setting while still seeing small fizzy bubbles at the edge. This is called simmering.

Stir-fry

Using a large frying-pan and a high heat, you quickly cook small items, stirring (or tossing) as you go. You use small items because they cook quickly. You can make a stir-fry using pretty much anything you fancy – for example, vegetables, meat, ham or prawns. You can flavour it with herbs, spices, lemon juice, balsamic vinegar, soy sauce or any bought stir-fry sauce. The limit is your imagination.

Sauces

It's well worth learning how to make some basic sauces, such as white sauce or cheese sauce. One very simple way of making the base of a sauce, or for thickening soups or casseroles, is to use cornflour with a little milk or water – follow the instructions on the packet. You can add grated chese, white wine, cider or a little mustard – any of these will give a good flavour. Never simply add any sort of flour to a bubbling casserole/soup etc. You'll end up with lumps.

Troubleshoot

➤ For further information about all aspects of food and kitchen safety and hygiene, visit www.food.gov.uk

➤ **The Vegetarian Society of the United Kingdom**
Parkdale
Dunham Road
Altrincham
Cheshire
England WA14 4QG
Tel: 0161 925 2000
www.vegsoc.org

➤ **The Vegan Society**
Donald Watson House
7 Battle Road
St Leonards-on-Sea
East Sussex TN37 7AA
Tel: 01424 427393
www.vegansociety.com

➤ **Some more recipe websites:**
www.allrecipes.com
www.bbc.co.uk/food/recipes
www.rachelsorganic.co.uk
www.seafish.org
www.recipes4us.co.uk

Health

Contents

Introduction 185

Don't get ill
in the first place   186
What about taking vitamin
   supplements? 188

Registering with a GP
. 190
How to register. 190
Questions and answers . .192
Prescriptions 193
What are your rights
   regarding your GP practice?
  196
Immunization/vaccination . .
  197
Contraception 198
Emergency contraception . . .
  198

Sexual health 200
The emotional side 200

In your medicine box
. . . . 201
Painkillers 201

Safe use of medicines
. . . . 203

Being ill 205
Where to get help 205
What is an emergency? . 206

Toxic shock syndrome
. . . . 208

Fever 209
What is a fever? 209
Taking your temperature 209
Reducing a fever. 210

Unpleasant but minor
. . . . 211
Colds and flu 211
Sickness/diarrhoea/food
   poisoning 215
Migraine or severe headache
   217

Other things you
should see a GP
about 219

First Aid 221

Minor first aid 222

Teeth 224

Registering with a dentist ...
.... 224

Dental emergencies 225

Eyes 226

How do I find an optician? ..
.... 226

Stress and happiness
.... 227

Troubleshoot 231

5

HEALTH

5

HEALTH

Introduction

When you lived at home, being ill was simple. Adults told you what was wrong with you, rushed out and bought medicines if necessary, decided if you needed a doctor, made the appointment, drove you there, drove you back, waited in the rain to collect the prescription, tucked you up in bed and brought you cool drinks or hot-water bottles and offered you tempting foods until you felt better. Well, something like that anyway. All you had to do was sleep, watch TV and make constant demands for sympathy and attention.

So, how do you cope now there's no handy forehead-mopping adult?

5

HEALTH

Don't get ill in the first place

Prevention is better than cure, they say. 'They' are right, though a healthy dose of realism comes in handy too – in other words, though there's a lot you *can* do to keep well, illness is an inevitable part of life, so at some point you *will* be ill.

I'll start by being optimistic though. What can you do to avoid being struck down by a bug every time you open your mouth?

➤ Keep your immune system strong. That's the highly complex (i.e. I can't explain it) system in your body which attacks and repels invaders like bacteria and viruses and possibly diseases such as cancer too. How do you keep it strong?

• Eat well. Fruit, veg and fortified cereals are all excellent for the immune system. 'Yuck, veg!' I hear you say. But you may be surprised how many ways there are to turn your least favourite vegetable into something truly enjoyable. There are ideas in the **Enjoying food** section: ➠ pages 169–74.

• Get some sunlight. This isn't about sunbathing, which we all know is, very annoyingly, bad for your skin and can be dangerous. But we do need some sunlight – apparently about fifteen minutes a day, even just on our hands, so that our bodies can produce vitamin D. So get outside for a while every day – the relevant light rays cannot penetrate glass.

• Exercise. Regular exercise is very important for health. It doesn't have to be utterly exhausting – but you should get up a light sweat (any way you want, so long as it doesn't involve hurting someone else or breaking the law) at least three times a week for 25–30 minutes. Walking, dancing and kicking a ball around are easy ways to do this. On top of that, try to walk instead of taking the lift or bus each day.

- Be happy. Easier said than done, of course, but it's very well known that your mood affects your immune system. If you are down, your body will be vulnerable to attack from all sorts of bugs.

- Avoid stress. Again, easy to say, but it's also very well known that too much stress is bad for your immune system (though a certain amount is no bad thing at all). One of the best ways to avoid stress is to take exercise. The other is to spend time with people who make you feel good and not people who drag you down. More about this in the **Stress and happiness** section: ➡ page 227.

- Smile, even if you don't feel happy. Fascinating research has shown that when we use our smile muscles, even if we feel grumpy as hell, we actually release chemicals called endorphins into our bodies – these are our natural happy drugs and make us feel good. Go and see a funny film.

➤ Practise good kitchen hygiene ➡ pages 162–8.

➤ Don't keep away from ill people. Er, surely some mistake? No, I mean it. OK, so there's a risk you might catch something, but actually it's not so likely unless they actually sneeze on you or are sick on you. As long as you take good precautions, such as washing your hands and keep the bathroom and sick room clean, you are actually doing your immune system a favour by exposing yourself to small quantities of bugs – your body can fight off small amounts and your immune system is then stronger. Also, your sick friend is much more likely to look after you when you get ill. Frankly, after making you ill, it's the least she/he can do.

➤ Get a flu vaccination if you need one. Apart from the very young and the elderly, healthy people do not normally need flu vaccinations. You can have one if you want one – ask your GP. Some chemists also offer flu vaccinations each winter, for a small fee. Many health professionals and especially alternative health professionals would say that a dose of flu is no bad thing for a normal healthy adult (though not exactly pleasant). *But*, if you have asthma, it *is* recommended that you have the vaccination. There are a few other categories of people with long-term health problems who should also have one – ask your GP.

➤ Be careful about where you eat out. It is possible to get food poisoning from even the most expensive restaurant and many cheap restaurants have perfect food hygiene. However, be suspicious of or avoid the following:

• Shellfish, unless you really trust the restaurant – a specialist fish restaurant, for example, ought to be a safe bet.

• Food that arrives at the table warm, when it should be hot.

• Food that looks as though it has been sitting around for a couple of hours at room temperature (i.e. neither in a chilled cabinet nor on a very hot plate).

• Mayonnaise, shellfish or poultry items from a buffet which is not properly chilled as it waits to be eaten.

• Food from a restaurant with obvious bad hygiene practices.

What about taking vitamin supplements?

Isn't that as good as eating fruit and veg?

No. Most nutrition experts say that vitamin tablets are not a good substitute for the real thing. There is also no real evidence that they prevent illness. You should get your nutrition from the food you eat. One exception is iron for people who are anaemic – but you would only know you needed it after a blood test and advice from a GP.

There are some supplements, however, which do seem to have some benefit. One is evening primrose oil, which can be useful for pre-menstrual syndrome (PMS). Cod-liver oil and Omega 3 fish oils are also very good for the immune system – though you wouldn't need it if you ate enough oily fish like herring, sardines and mackerel. Most people in the UK don't eat enough of those things nowadays.

Registering with a GP

Don't wait to get ill. One of the first things to do once you have found your new accommodation is register with a GP (and dentist ➡ page 224).

Everyone has a right to register free with a National Health Service (NHS) GP. All your medical treatment and appointments will be free (though this may change in the future). A GP will arrange hospital visits if you require further tests or treatment. Normally, you must register with a GP close to where you live – because occasionally your GP may need to come to visit you and obviously he/she should not have to spend valuable time travelling unnecessarily.

There is usually more than one doctor working at the same surgery or health centre. A group of doctors working together is called a 'practice', so you may hear people talk about a particular GP practice.

> **NOTE:** If someone talks about a 'private GP', this means that this is not within the NHS and is therefore not free.

How to register

➤ Choose a GP practice or health centre near you: either use the phone book (Yellow Pages) or ask neighbours whom they use or recommend. There can be differences between GP practices. For example, you might prefer the choice of a female or male doctor; some practices have longer waiting-lists for routine appointments; some practices offer special services such as homeopathy or acupuncture, which will usually be free to patients registered at that practice – you would pay a lot for such treatments in private practices. For websites which will help you find a local GP, ➥ **Troubleshoot** section on page 231.

➤ Phone or visit – visiting is a good idea as you can then *see* the sort of services offered simply by looking at the posters and notices. If you think it will suit you, ask if you can be registered.

- They may say yes. At this point, they will ask for your address and your NHS medical card. Don't worry if you don't have one – you will simply be asked to fill out a form and a card will be sent to you. You do not have to bring the card with you to each appointment and it is not a disaster if you lose it, but you may occasionally need to tell someone your NHS number so try to keep it safe.

- They may say no if they don't have space for you. They may *not* refuse you because of age, colour, race, religion, sexual orientation or existing illness. You should therefore not give these details until you have discovered whether they have space.

- If they don't have space, try other local practices. If you can't find one that will take you, phone your local Primary Care Trust (PCT) – they are obliged to find you a GP. You will find your local PCT number in the Yellow Pages, under Health Authorities and Services. ➥ **Troubleshoot** section on page 231.

➤ That's it! Once you are registered, keep a note of the GP's phone number where you can easily find it. And ask about the system for making appointments – different practices can have quite different systems. Some don't have an appointment system – you just turn up.

Questions and answers

Question: If I haven't registered with a GP, does this mean I can't get treatment?

Answer: No. A GP must treat you if you are ill. However, you will have to fill out a form as a visitor. The real problem is that the GP won't have any of your medical records, which are very important when it comes to deciding what is the best treatment for you. So, do register as soon as you can. Also, if you have any existing conditions, such as asthma, your new GP can quickly receive all your old notes and you will not have to explain everything from the start.

Question: What happens if I register and then find I really don't like my GP or I wish I had chosen another one?

Answer: You have the right to change GP without giving a reason. But before going through the process of registering with a different practice, see if there's a different GP in the same practice whom you might perhaps prefer to see.

If you do decide to change practices, check first whether you can find another practice which has room for you. If you decide you want to change, tell your new GP you want to do so, and he/she will arrange for everything to be transferred from the old one. It can take many weeks for notes to be moved.

Question: There are several GPs in my practice and on my medical card it says I am registered with just one of them. What happens if I want to see a different one in the same practice?

Answer: That is absolutely no problem. You will automatically be registered with one GP but you can ask to see anyone you like in the same practice. They all have access to your records. When you phone for an appointment, just say, 'I'd like to make an appointment with Dr Blah, please.' Sometimes a particular GP has a speciality – in this case, the GP you see may suggest you see another one.

Question: Will the doctor come to see me at home if I am ill?

Answer: Only if it is impossible for you to come to the surgery. If at all possible, don't ask for a home visit because a doctor can see many more patients in the surgery than by doing home visits. When you phone the practice, the receptionist may question you closely about why you need a home visit. But, if you *really* cannot come to the surgery because you are too ill, don't be afraid to say so.

Question: I was really worried I might be pregnant so I phoned for an appointment and the receptionist asked if it was an emergency, urgent or routine – I didn't know how to answer.

Answer: If you are worried about something, simply say that it is something you are really worried about and you want to see someone as soon as possible. The receptionist only asks these questions to try to provide the best service for everyone and to allow spaces for genuine emergencies. If you can explain the nature of the problem to the receptionist, this makes it easier, but if you feel she/he is being unsympathetic and you really are more worried than she/he realizes, do say so. It is your health and, frankly, the NHS is there to serve you.

Prescriptions

Prescription-only drugs

Some drugs can only be prescribed by a doctor or dentist. These include most antibiotics (in the UK). If your GP thinks you should have one of these, he or she will write the details on a piece of paper; you take it to a shop which says 'dispensing chemist' or 'dispensing pharmacist'; the pharmacist gives you the correct drug with the correct instructions for you (which may be different from the instructions someone else got for the same drug).

Do I have to pay for a prescription?

➤ No   If you are under 16; or under 19 and in full-time education.

➤ No   If you are pregnant.

➤ No   If you are over 60 (in which case, you are rather old to be leaving home for the first time).

➤ No   If you are receiving Income Support, Jobseeker's Allowance, Working Families Tax Credit, Disabled Person's Tax Credit.

➤ No   If you have one of a small number of medical conditions – your GP should tell you and you will be able to get a special medical exemption certificate. This will mean that *all* your prescriptions are free, even those unconnected to your condition. Examples of such conditions are epilepsy, diabetes (insulin-dependent) and an underactive thyroid. Asthma is *not* a qualifying condition. (But: ➡ **Pre-paid certificate** on page 195.)

➤ Yes   If you come into any other category.

NOTE: All contraception is free through the NHS – either through your GP or through any NHS Family Planning clinic. Emergency contraception is also free, as long as you go through an NHS clinic or GP practice (➡ pages 198–9).

If you are on a low income, you may be exempt, even if you do not come into one of the exempt categories above. It is worth asking your GP how to go about this.

Pre-paid certificate

If you think you will have to pay for more than five prescription items in four months or fourteen items in twelve months, you may find it cheaper to buy a pre-payment certificate (PPC). From 1 April 2005 a four-month PPC will cost you £33.90 and a twelve-month PPC £93.20. This means that you pay nothing more, however many prescriptions you need. If, for example, you have asthma and you use two different inhalers (which is very common for asthmatics), your GP will only usually give you a prescription for two months at a time. That's two prescriptions, six times a year. If you also have eczema or get a throat infection, you could well find yourself saving money with a PPC.

Ask at a pharmacy for details of how to get one.

Over-the-counter (OTC)

OTC drugs are those which you can buy without a prescription. They will be behind the pharmacist's counter and you will have to ask for them. This is because the pharmacist or assistant has to ask you certain questions or tell you something important about the drug. For example, she/he might need to ask if you are asthmatic or if you are allergic to something. You should always be honest about your answers. The pharmacist can also give you advice about which is the best one for you.

OTC on prescription

If you do not normally pay for prescriptions, your GP can write you a prescription for an OTC drug. Then you will not have to pay for it. On the other hand, if you *do* pay for prescriptions, the drug which the GP wants you to have *may* be cheaper bought OTC, because a prescription is a fixed price (currently £6.50 per drug in April 2005) but an OTC drug may be cheaper. Be sure to tell the GP whether you do or don't pay for prescriptions.

What are your rights regarding your GP practice?

Your GP/nurse must not:

➤ tell anyone what you tell him or her, except another medical practitioner who will be involved in your care;

➤ tell your parents, teachers or carers anything, unless you specifically authorize it;

➤ carry out any test or procedure without your permission and without explaining fully any risks;

➤ watch while you are getting undressed;

➤ try out any untested or unauthorized drugs on you;

➤ enter you in a drug trial without your informed consent;

➤ discriminate against you on the basis of your sex, sexual orientation, religion or wealth.

Your GP/nurse should:

➤ act in *your* best interests at all times;

➤ explain your treatment in a way that you can understand, so that you can make choices about tests and treatment;

➤ treat you with respect and dignity;

➤ treat all your medical records confidentially. The receptionists are also obliged to treat all your information completely confidentially;

➤ allow you access to your health records;

➤ call you for routine checks such as a smear test (for women – usually every three years. Don't miss it. Two minutes of minor embarrassment, that's all it is);

➤ ensure that a chaperone of the same sex as you is available during any personal examination carried out by a GP or nurse. If one is not there and you would like one, do ask.

HEALTH

IMPORTANT NOTE: You should also take responsibility for any routine tests you require, as the automatic recall system does not always work. Women should have a smear test every three years, for example. If you have not had one, do ask.

IMPORTANT NOTE: If you make an appointment, make sure you keep it. If you get better or decide that you don't need the appointment, PHONE the practice immediately. They can then offer the space to someone who needs it. You could be blacklisted if you repeatedly miss appointments.

Immunization/vaccination

When you register with a GP, you will be asked to come for a health check, probably with the practice nurse. You will be weighed and measured and asked about your previous health. You will also be asked whether your immunizations are up-to-date. You will probably have had immunizations as a baby and child, and boosters again at 15. Don't worry if you are not sure about this, as the nurse will tell you what to do or how to find out.

The main one that you will probably be asked about is tetanus, as this is one which requires a booster occasionally through your life. Tetanus is a dangerous disease which can be picked up through the soil – for example, if you cut your foot and then walk barefoot. If in doubt, accept another booster – it could save your life. Also, if you have a bad cut at any time or are severely scratched by an animal and you have not had a recent tetanus booster, make an appointment for one. Tetanus is rare, thanks to this programme of vaccination, but it is something you should be aware of and prevent.

If you are going abroad, ask at your GP's practice whether you need any special injections. Most are free, apart from the cost of the prescription.

Contraception

Also called family planning – even though a family is probably the last thing you are planning. As you know, you can buy condoms at a pharmacist and in lots of supermarkets. However, you do not need to pay for contraception – if you go through your GP or a family planning clinic or any NHS funded health centre, all contraception is free. It is also completely confidential.

For more information ➡ the helplines listed on page 199.

Emergency contraception

If you have had unprotected sex (sex without contraception), taking emergency contraception will usually prevent pregnancy. You might be worried that your contraception might have failed, perhaps because a condom split or you forgot to take your pill.

People often refer to the 'morning-after pill', but this is misleading because it can be effective several days after sex. There are two types of emergency contraception:

> **Emergency pills**
> You take these pills within three days of unprotected sex, but they are more effective the earlier you take them.
> **An IUD** (intrauterine device)
> This must be fitted within five days of unprotected sex.

Things to remember

> Emergency contraception is free on prescription (from any GP surgery, NHS clinic, Young People's or Brook clinic).
> You can buy it from some pharmacists.
> It is safe.
> Treatment is confidential.
> Almost every woman can use one of the methods – even if you can't take the regular pill.
> There is no time limit to the number of times you can take it.

➤ You can take it twice in one cycle.
➤ It is not as effective as using other methods of contraception regularly.
➤ Don't delay – see someone as soon as possible.
➤ Do not use a pill that was prescribed for someone else.

For more information call the Family Planning Association helplines.

England and Wales: 0845 3101334 (9 a.m. – 6 p.m.)
Scotland: 0141 5765088 (9 a.m. – 5 p.m.)
N Ireland: 02890 325 488 (9 a.m. – 5 p.m.)
Visit the website at www.fpa.org.uk.

5

HEALTH

Sexual health

The most important thing to remember about sexual health is that if you have unprotected sex with someone who may have had unprotected sex with someone else, you risk catching and/or passing on a sexually transmitted disease (STD). This can be anything from chlamydia to HIV/Aids. If you have only had sex with one person and he/she has never had sex with anyone apart from you, you are OK – but how can you be 100% sure that your partner is telling the truth?

Remember: for sex to be protected, you need to be using a *barrier* method of contraception. The pill does not protect you against STDs. A condom is the safest method.

For details about chlamydia, the most common STD, go to http://www.netdoctor.co.uk/diseases/facts/chlamydia.htm. It is a common infection which presents no symptoms until permanent damage is done. Men and women suffer it and you do *not* have to be promiscuous to contract it. You should not be ashamed – just aware. It is easily treatable if caught early.

Visit your GP or a Young People's or Brook clinic for information.

The emotional side

If you are worried or upset about any aspect of sex or your own sexuality, talk to someone. If you are a student, your student welfare officer can advise you where to go. Your GP will be very happy to help, by talking to you or advising you about other people you can talk to.

The Samaritans will also be able to help and tell you where to find specific help for you. Their number is on page 262.

In your medicine box

These are useful items to keep at home. After all, the last thing you feel like doing when you are ill is going out to buy medicine. Also, many minor illnesses are better if treated at the very first signs.

➤ Paracetamol/aspirin/ibuprofen – for pain or fever
➤ Anti-diarrhoea tablets or kaolin mixture
➤ Rehydration mixture
➤ Indigestion remedy or liver salts (often helpful for nausea or a hangover)
➤ Rescue Remedy cream (brilliant for minor burns and small injuries)
➤ A thermometer
➤ Sharp scissors and tweezers
➤ Selection of plasters, cotton wool
➤ Antiseptic cream or lotion
➤ Echinacea (➡ page 214)
➤ Essential oils, ideally lavender, lemon, tea tree, lemon and peppermint.

> **!** **WARNING:** Keep everything in a place where you can find it easily but children can *never* find it. A high cupboard is better than a locked drawer – you might leave a drawer unlocked by mistake.

Painkillers

Paracetamol, aspirin and ibuprofen all work against pain, fever and inflammation. However, aspirin and ibuprofen can irritate the stomach, so avoid them if you also feel sick or have indigestion. Aspirin is also not recommended for people with asthma.

It is fine to take paracetamol *and* aspirin together for severe pain, or paracetamol *and* ibuprofen. However, do *not* take aspirin *and* ibuprofen.

Safe use of medicines

➤ Always read instructions carefully: there is often very important information in the leaflet inside the packet. Don't throw the leaflet away.

➤ Never take more than the recommended dose.

➤ Never take something which has been prescribed for someone else.

➤ When medicines reach their use-by date, take them back to a pharmacy, where they will dispose of them safely.

➤ If a doctor gives you antibiotics, *always* finish the whole course, even if you feel completely better – this does not apply to other medicines, but ask a pharmacist if you are not sure.

➤ If you take more than one medicine, check that some of the ingredients are not repeated. Paracetamol is especially important because it appears in many medicines and is dangerous taken in quantities which are even *moderately* more than the stated dose. If you are not sure whether two medicines can go together, ask a pharmacist.

➤ Tell your doctor about any side effects, even if they seem quite minor. (No need to make an urgent appointment for this, unless they are severe and are stopping you from taking the medicine.)

➤ Tell your doctor or pharmacist if you are taking any other remedies, even herbal or homeopathic ones. Occasionally, these should not be taken together.

➤ You may be told not to drink alcohol while on certain drugs. Someone else may tell you there's no need to worry. But with *some* drugs, it is *very* important not to drink alcohol. With some antibiotics, you will be extremely sick if you drink while you are on them. Do obey instructions on the packet or given to you by the pharmacist or doctor.

Being ill

Being ill is horrible. It's very easy to think you are dying. If you have a temperature, for example, or a splitting headache, it's very easy to convince yourself that you have meningitis, or that you are about to be one of the very rare cases of people who die suddenly from what seems like simple flu. In your frightened mind, any severe stomach pain becomes appendicitis or cancer and recurring headaches simply must be a brain tumour. Especially at night, these fears seem all too real. You're not being stupid – we've all done it.

Relax: your symptoms are highly unlikely to be anything so serious. But it's very important to know exactly what symptoms you should worry about and which you should not.

Where to get help

➤ Pharmacy – your local chemist or pharmacist can give expert advice, recommend treatment and tell you if you should see a doctor.

➤ GP – for long-term problems and worries, things that are not immediate emergencies, such as general illness, or fears about a lump/mole, or moderate pain that does not go away after a day or so, make an appointment with your GP.

➤ NHS Direct/NHS24 – if you are worried and don't know if it is an emergency or not, phone NHS Direct on 0845 4647 (England and Wales) or NHS24 on 08454 242424 (Scotland). You will be put through to a fully qualified nurse who can listen to your symptoms and tell you what to do. They are open day and night, every day of the year. They will call an ambulance for you if necessary and give both emergency and long-term advice.

➤ NHS Direct website – www.nhsdirect.co.uk – here you can input your symptoms and receive instant advice as to what you should do. You can also find out about virtually any illness or medical problem you can imagine.

➤ Walk-In Injury Clinic – if you need immediate treatment but it is not life-threatening – for example, if you have sprained a joint badly, or burnt or cut yourself – a Walk-In Injury Clinic could be the best bet, if you are lucky enough to have one near you. You do not need an appointment; they are open 7 a.m. till 10 p.m. seven days a week and you will usually be seen more quickly than if you take a minor injury to an A&E department. For your nearest one ➡ the **Troubleshoot** section on page 231.

➤ A&E (Accident and Emergency Department) In an emergency, either go to A&E in a taxi or get a friend to drive you, or call an ambulance by dialling 999. Don't drive yourself. If in doubt call an ambulance – only take the taxi/car option if you do not have an immediately life-threatening condition. Ambulance personnel can begin treatment as soon as they reach you. You can't just turn up to any old hospital – some don't have an A&E department. Check where your nearest one is *before* you have an emergency.

What is an emergency?

There are certain symptoms which you should treat as an emergency. These mean you should get to A&E straight away, by ambulance if this is the quickest way to get attention. These symptoms should not be ignored – even though in many cases they may turn out to be nothing life-threatening. Having these symptoms does *not* mean you are dying – it simply means you need expert assessment immediately and treatment to prevent them developing.

999 Dial 999 if you or somebody with you has any of these symptoms:

➤ Unconsciousness, even if brief; drowsiness
➤ Deep wound
➤ Heavy blood loss, even if it has now stopped
➤ Suspected broken bone
➤ Suspected heart attack
➤ Breathing difficulties
➤ Severe/sudden allergic reaction – e.g. swollen throat, tongue, lips, fainting or trouble breathing
➤ Severe burns
➤ A rash which does not fade when you press a glass on the skin
➤ Severe headache accompanied by vomiting or fever (➤ **Fever** on page 209) and a stiff or painful neck

The final two symptoms are possible signs of meningitis, and it is essential to get to hospital straight away. (➤ **Meningitis** on page 300.)

HEALTH

Toxic shock syndrome

This is a serious condition, usually associated with using a tampon, though around half the cases reported each year occur in people not using them, including men and children. If toxic shock syndrome is not recognized early it can be fatal, though most otherwise healthy people do make a full recovery.

If you develop any of these symptoms while you are wearing a tampon, remove it and see a doctor immediately: high fever, a rash, vomiting, diarrhoea, a sore throat, dizziness or fainting. They are similar to flu symptoms. You will reduce the risk of TSS by always using a tampon correctly. The packet has full instructions, so do remind yourself of these before you next use one.

Without wanting to joke about these things, obviously I realize that you can't make a phone call if you are unconscious. Also, confusion or drowsiness may make you unable to take these decisions. If you are on your own and begin to feel any of these symptoms quite mildly, have a friend with you in case you become worse. Then the friend can decide. If in doubt, phone NHS Direct.

For more information on dealing with medical emergencies, ➥ page 284.

Fever

What is a fever?

The normal, healthy internal human body temperature is around 37°C (98.4°F), give or take half a degree. With certain illnesses, your temperature may rise as your body fights off the infection. If your temperature rises above 37.5°C or 38°C, you will begin to feel ill and this is regarded as a fever.

A fever of 39°C (102.2°F) is regarded as a high fever and you will certainly feel very unwell. Any higher than this and you may also experience some confusion. At this point, you should really have someone with you, to reassure you and to help you get your fever down.

Taking your temperature

You need a medical thermometer. Place it in your mouth under your tongue and gently close your mouth. Leave it there for at least one minute.

If you have just had a hot bath or a hot drink, or if you have just done vigorous exercise, this may give a falsely high reading. Also, natural temperature tends to be a little higher in the evening. Finally, for women, there are slight differences in temperature depending on the time of the menstrual cycle. Do not worry about half a degree here or there.

HEALTH

Reducing a fever

➤ Take aspirin (unless you are allergic or have asthma) or paracetamol.

➤ Keep fluid levels high by drinking plenty of water or juice; avoid hot drinks or very cold drinks.

➤ Remove excess clothing or bedding, but do not allow yourself to become cold.

➤ Pat your skin with wet, tepid (blood temperature) cloths – do not use cold water or ice because this actually makes your blood vessels and pores tighten, stopping the heat from escaping from your body.

If you are worried, phone NHS Direct and explain your symptoms as well as the exact temperature you have.

5

HEALTH

Unpleasant but minor

Once you are happy that none of your symptoms fall into the 'emergency' category, what do you do? Below are a few of the minor and common illnesses and their treatments.

The best doctor for a minor illness is your own body. Your immune system is designed to fight off all the bugs which attack it. In fact, the unpleasant symptoms are actually caused by your body's immune system in action and many health experts believe that the best thing to do is not interfere with your body's natural strength. By letting it fight for itself, you make your immune system stronger the next time it is attacked.

On the other hand, it's a weird person who says, 'Bring on the pain – I want to suffer.' So, on that basis, let's look at what you can safely do to make yourself feel better and get better quickly.

Colds and flu

Colds and flu are both caused by viruses, but they are not the same. Doctors rightly get irritated by people saying they've got flu when it's just a bad cold. There are hundreds of different cold viruses and a whole army of different flu ones and how ill you feel will depend on a) which one attacks you and b) how well your body fights it off.

Symptoms

Cold or flu? In short, if you can struggle on, despite feeling as though your head is stuffed with cheese, and perhaps with a day of really wanting to go to bed and die, it is a cold. If you have *several* days of feeling completely hellish and pretty out of it, with no choice but to stay in bed, it is probably flu. With flu, you will feel ill for at least a week.

In detail: well, you know what a cold is like. Flu has some of the same symptoms (sometimes including the runny/blocked nose, sore throat and cough) but some extra ones as well:

> a fever (➡ **Fever**, page 209). Actually, you can often have a mild fever with an ordinary cold, too, but a high fever (39°C or higher) indicates something more, and quite likely flu;

> aching joints;

> moderately severe headache, especially when you stand up or raise your eyes;

> feeling sick or even being sick; you will probably not feel like eating.

> **WARNING:** If the headache and/or sickness are severe, and are accompanied by a stiff or painful neck, or you have a rash which does not fade when a glass is pressed to it, or if you feel very confused, seek emergency medical attention.

Self-treatment

> Rest – listen to your body. This is particularly important with genuine flu. If you try to struggle on and do too much, you can delay your recovery. You could even risk something called 'post-viral fatigue', which is when a virus lingers on and on for weeks or months because your body was not allowed to fight it off. However, the longer you stay in bed, the weaker your muscles become, so with any illness you should get up as soon as you can and keep your muscles working. Avoid strenuous exercise until you really feel like it. Be very kind to yourself.

> Paracetamol – very effective for pain relief (e.g. from throat/head) and also for reducing fever. **DO NOT TAKE**

MORE THAN THE RECOMMENDED DOSE.
(➡ **Safe use of Medicines,** page 203.)

➤ OTC remedies – there are many OTC (over-the-counter ➡ page 195) remedies for colds and flu. Most of them have paracetamol in so you must *not* take separate paracetamol as well. Lots have lemon, blackcurrant or honey in. These are soothing, but will be unlikely to make your cold go away or get better faster.

➤ Essential oils (often called aromatherapy oils) – there are several oils that may make your symptoms feel better. Eucalyptus, lavender, lemon and tea tree are useful for many ailments. Some are not cheap, though, and if I had to choose two I'd have lavender and either lemon or tea tree. (They must be described as pure essential oils – cheap is definitely nasty in this case.)

   • Lavender is the only one you can put directly on your skin. Some drops on your pillow or tissue can help you sleep. A drop rubbed into the glands of your neck is very soothing. Lavender is strongly antibacterial and can be useful for treating and even preventing some bacterial infections such as throat infections. Try gargling with warm water that has a couple of drops of lavender oil in it. (Don't swallow it.)

   • A couple of drops of lemon or tea tree oil in a cup of warm water and then gargled can also be great for sore throats, especially if you do it at the very first sign of soreness or roughness. Tea tree is thought to be powerfully anti-viral. You should dilute it in warm water or almond oil before putting it on your skin. You can also put a few drops in a bath. Do not swallow it – though obviously a tiny amount will remain in your mouth after gargling. This will not do you any harm, but you aren't supposed to swallow it and should never use it undiluted externally or internally.

   • A few drops of eucalyptus in a bowl of just-boiled water

5

HEALTH

makes a great nose-clearing steam inhalation. Place the bowl on a firm table and sit over it with a towel over your head. Close your eyes and breathe deeply through your nose (if possible…) for as long as you can bear it.

➤ Echinacea – this natural remedy has become very popular in recent years and many people swear by it. I am one of them and will simply say I haven't had a cold since I started to use it about five years ago. I simply take it at the first hint that a cold might be on its way – a sore or rough throat, for example. Other people take it most of the time – but I don't see the point in taking a treatment when there's no illness, even if the treatment is 'natural'. Even the manufacturers do not recommend constant use. It'll cost you a fortune too – whereas taking it for a couple of days at a time will not break the bank and will be worth it if it knocks a cold dead or even makes the symptoms less bad.

➤ Drink plenty of fluids. Illness makes you sweat and it's really important not to become dehydrated. Avoid alcohol and coffee as they make you lose more fluid. Stick to water or diluted juice as often as you can manage it.

➤ Reduce fever ➡ **Fever** page 209.

➤ Don't eat if you don't feel like it.

When to see a GP or seek further help from NHS Direct/NHS24

➤ (NHS24) If your fever rises above 39°C/102.2°F.

➤ (GP) If your very sore throat has white spots on it. This probably means a throat infection, perhaps tonsillitis. Not life-threatening, but antibiotics will deal with it.

➤ (NHS24) If you have any of the symptoms mentioned in the emergency list on page 300.

➤ (GP) If you develop a cough which is painful or produces phlegm – you may have a chest infection, in which case the doctor will treat this very easily with antibiotics.

Question: I had an appalling cough and felt hellish. My friend said I probably needed antibiotics so I went to the doctor but the doctor didn't give me any. Why?

Answer: Because antibiotics are for infections caused by bacteria and your doctor decided you did not have such an infection. You can have a bad cough as a result of the cold virus, for example. Antibiotics do not work against viruses and it would be a bad idea to take them. If your cough changes and becomes more chesty, painful or produces phlegm, return to your doctor – it may be that it has now turned into an infection.

Sickness/diarrhoea/food poisoning

Symptoms
Well, pretty obvious really. Let's not go into them too closely!

Self-treatment
Whether your sickness and diarrhoea is caused by a bug you caught from someone else or by a food poisoning organism, it will almost always get better without help. Usually, you will be feeling much better within 24–48 hours. But there are some things you can do to help.

➤ Try to keep your fluid intake up. Of course, if you cannot keep even water down, this is difficult. It's important to drink, so just sip it gradually. Avoid alcohol, coffee, neat juice and milk – stick to water or weak diluting juice.

➤ Rehydration. The problem with having sickness and diarrhoea is not so much the fluid you lose – it's the salts and sugar from your body. You can combat this by buying an OTC rehydration mixture which you mix with water and sip. However, if your symptoms have eased after not more than 24 hours, reintroducing your normal diet will soon have you back to normal and there is no need to do anything further.

➤ Peppermint essential oil is a powerful anti-nausea treatment. Add one drop of pure oil to a cup of hot water. It won't mix in properly so you have to keep stirring it constantly. Drink tiny sips. If you feel too sick to drink it, even smelling it and inhaling it can really help. Warning: it's very strong so don't let the neat oil touch your lips. Also, shut your eyes, as peppermint steam is seriously eye-watering!

➤ Ginger is another excellent and natural remedy for nausea. You can take it in any form you fancy: sip 'dry' ginger ale, nibble ginger biscuits, or even chew a piece of fresh ginger – phone a friend to go and get you what you need.

➤ Until symptoms disappear, avoid eating anything spicy, anything rich and creamy or fatty, as well as acidic fruit (such as apples, oranges and tomatoes), most veg and bran. Introduce bland foods, such as toast, potatoes or biscuits, gradually and don't return to your normal diet until all your symptoms have gone. Bananas are excellent, as they contain potassium, which is one of the most important elements lost during sickness and diarrhoea.

Hygiene

Sickness and diarrhoea can easily be passed around everyone in your house if you don't take simple precautions.

➤ Wash your hands properly with soap and hot water every time you use the toilet.

➤ Use your own towel and your own cups/crockery, etc.

➤ Clean the toilet properly.

➤ Do not prepare food for other people while you have symptoms of illness.

When to see a GP or seek further help from NHS Direct

➤ If you do not start to feel better after 48 hours or if you feel worse after 24 hours.

➤ If you have severe stomach pains for more than a few hours – especially if the pain is constant instead of cramp-like or spasmodic.

➤ If you also have a fever (➡ **Fever**, page 209).

➤ If you are being sick for more than 24 hours and/or become too weak to look after yourself.

➤ If you start to be drowsy or delirious.

Migraine or severe headache

Symptoms

What's the difference? Most people can continue working or going about their daily business with a headache. With a migraine you usually can't. With a migraine, it's hard to do anything other than lie down in a darkened room – which is the best thing to do, if possible.

Self-treatment

➤ There are lots of OTC remedies. Most are based on either paracetamol or aspirin or ibuprofen. The best thing to do is ask a pharmacist what might work better for your own symptoms – and then make sure you always have some in the house. If you feel sick, it's best to avoid ibuprofen and aspirin as they can sometimes irritate your stomach, especially if you haven't eaten. There are also special OTC remedies for migraine, usually containing something to deal with nausea as well as pain.

➤ Relax – many headaches are caused by tension. If you can relax the muscles in your neck, face, jaw and shoulders, this can help.

➤ Acupressure – this works on the same principle as

acupuncture but there are no needles. You can also treat yourself. The pressure points for headaches are at the very tip of your big toe and also in the fleshy bit where your thumb joins your hand. Press one of these spots quite hard, with a circular motion, for several seconds.

➤ Consider the possibility that your migraines are related to a food intolerance. Eliminate a possible food culprit and see if that helps. Common culprits seem to be chocolate, cheese, red wine, wheat and dairy produce. Start by eliminating one and see if you get a migraine over the next few weeks. You could see a dietician for help with this – though you will have to pay if your GP can't refer you to one.

NOTE: Paying for allergy testing is possible, though many GPs would not advise this. It is often unreliable and may be expensive. Food intolerances, as opposed to genuine allergies, are notoriously difficult to identify.

When to see a GP or seek further help from NHS Direct

(Also ➥ **Meningitis** on page 300.)

➤ If your headache is very severe indeed and is accompanied by a stiff or painful neck or inability to look at the light.

➤ If you very often wake up with a headache which soon gets better as the day goes on.

➤ If your severe headache is accompanied by drowsiness or confusion.

➤ If your headache is accompanied by severe sickness and you think it is more than a migraine.

Other things you should see a GP about

➤ A lump anywhere on your body, whether painful or not, which has been there for a week. Most lumps will be nothing to worry about, but a few may need attention.

➤ A mole which has changed or begun to worry you. Itching, bleeding or changing shape are signs you should look for. Again, most changes turn out to be unimportant but no doctor will *ever* think you are silly to have a mole checked. You can ask to have it removed even if the GP says it is nothing to worry about.

➤ Any skin lesion which looks odd – it could be a red mark that won't disappear, or anything that won't heal. Again, almost certainly nothing to worry about, but definitely important to check. Even if any of these things do turn out to be something nasty, they will be very easy to treat if caught early enough.

➤ Bleeding from your rectum/anus; blood in your stools – by the way, 'stools' is the word your GP will use for what comes out of your rear end, so don't look confused and think he/she is talking about your kitchen furniture.

➤ Any symptom at all which persists for more than a couple of weeks or keeps recurring – headaches, dizziness, abdominal pains, joint pains, anything.

➤ Anything which keeps you awake at night worrying about it – nine times out of ten, your doctor will reassure you. In the other one time out of ten, you will need some further tests and the earlier these can be done the better. So don't delay – that's what your GP is there for.

➤ Any illness that does not show signs of improvement

during the time it normally takes people to recover. Or any illness that was getting better but then gets worse.

TIP: Before your appointment, write down the things you want to tell your GP. It's very easy to forget once you are in the surgery. Tell your GP things even if you are not sure if they are relevant. However, remember that a routine appointment may only last ten minutes (or less), so try to use the time efficiently.

TIP: When seeing a GP, don't be embarrassed about anything. The doctor will have seen or heard it all before. And remember – what goes on in the GP's or nurse's consulting room does *not* get talked about outside. Breaking confidentiality is a disciplinary offence for a doctor, nurse or receptionist.

TIP: All cancers are much more easily treated if detected early. It is really important for women to examine their breasts and men their testicles once a month. (Actually, men can get breast cancer, so a lump there should also be investigated.) That way, if you find a lump, you know it has only been there a short while and if you need treatment, it will be much easier. Remember that most lumps will not be serious, but all should be investigated further. For details of how to examine yourself and what to look for, ask at your GP surgery for a leaflet, or visit http://www.cancerresearchuk.org. (Navigate to 'About Cancer', then 'Specific Cancers'.)

First aid

More than 4000 people die in accidents in the home and 2.8 million are injured in the UK every year. You could do you and your friends a huge service by doing a short first aid course. Ask at your GP's practice for details of a course near you. You could even save a life.

Real emergencies are covered in the Emergency section of this book, ➡ from page 284.

This book can cover only the most ordinary and common accidents. I strongly advise you to buy a good and simple first aid book and to take a course in basic first aid. It will save you a lot of panic if something happens. The examples that follow assume that someone else has the injury and you are the one giving first aid. It may be that *you* are the victim and are on your own – try to do the same things to yourself, and get help if necessary.

5

HEALTH

Minor first aid

Bleeding wound

- Press a clean, thick pad onto the wound and keep pressing.
- Raise the bleeding limb so that it is higher than the heart.
- Press firmly on the area above the wound, for 10 seconds at a time.
- Get help if bleeding continues: **see your GP, phone NHS Direct or call 999**.
- If bleeding stops but the edges of the wound are open, it may need stitching: **see your GP or phone NHS Direct.**
- Keep the patient still and calm. If she/he experiences dizziness, **phone NHS Direct**.
- DO NOT put water on the wound.
- DO NOT tie a tourniquet to stop blood flow to the wound – you can cause damage to the limb like this.
- DO NOT give the patient alcohol – it makes blood flow faster.

Minor head injury

- Treat even a brief loss of consciousness seriously. **Call 999.**
- Watch out for: drowsiness, confusion, vomiting. **Call 999 or call NHS Direct.**
- Watch out for the above symptoms up to 36 hours after a head injury, even if there was no loss of consciousness.
- DO NOT give alcohol or food/drink if there has been loss of consciousness or any of the symptoms mentioned above.

For severe head injury, ➡ page 298.

Burns

➤ Run under cold water for 15 minutes if possible.

➤ Remove any rings, jewellery or tight clothing near the burn (if possible).

➤ For small burns without broken skin/blistering, apply Rescue cream generously – but not if the burn is larger than the victim's hand.

➤ For a burn larger than the victim's hand, **call NHS Direct or see your GP.**

➤ If the victim suffers dizziness, confusion or clamminess, **call 999 or NHS Direct.**

➤ Cover the wound in clingfilm or a non-fluffy clean cloth (e.g. a hankie).

➤ Give paracetamol.

➤ Get help if the condition worsens, **call 999 or NHS Direct.**

➤ Keep the victim calm and quiet afterwards. **Phone NHS Direct if you are concerned.**

The greatest danger with even quite small burns is infection. Keep the area covered with clingfilm or a clean dressing until seen by a doctor

Teeth

Registering with a dentist

Also very important, but often more difficult, is registering with a dentist. The reason it is more difficult is that that many dentists now do not do NHS work. You may phone many dentists before you find one with space. You may not find one at all – they may only take private patients. This can be very expensive indeed.

What to do

➤ First, phone one or more dentists and ask if they are registering new NHS patients. ➡ **Troubleshoot** for how to find one. Unlike doctors, you do *not* have to live very close so you do have a wider area to choose from. If you find one that can take you, it's very easy from then on. You will be asked to come for a check-up; the dentist may well want to see previous dental records – you'll need to get them from the dentist you used to see when you were at home. From then on, you will be sent a reminder (usually every 6–9 months) to make an appointment for a check-up. Do make the appointment – fifteen minutes of having someone poke around in your mouth is much better than letting cavities form and causing great pain later.

➤ You will not have to pay if you are under 18 or if you are 18 and in full-time education. (In Wales, you do not pay for check-ups if you are under 25, though you will pay for treatment.) If you have a low income, you also may not need to pay. If you think this may include you, get a form called HC1 from a local benefit office, NHS hospital, dentist, optician or pharmacist. There is no harm in asking.

> **NOTE:** Even NHS dental treatment is not completely free. Costs are currently:
>
> Routine six-monthly examination £5.64
>
> Scale and polish £8.88
>
> Medium-sized silver amalgam filling £11.40

Dental problems

➤ Pain – make an appointment as soon as possible. Say you are in pain. Meanwhile, take paracetamol. A hot water bottle wrapped in a towel and held against your cheek can help, but won't deal with the cause. Prolonged pain may mean an abscess, which needs treatment.

➤ Broken tooth or dislodged filling – make an appointment as soon as possible. If you are in pain, say so.

➤ Accident which moves a tooth – see a dentist as soon as possible. If the tooth comes out, replace it in your mouth if possible, or keep it in a small container of milk. Make an emergency appointment or go to a dental hospital.

Dental hospitals have emergency clinics – find the number of yours now.

Eyes

It's important to look after your eyes. An eye check from an optician can also reveal other important illnesses. Most opticians charge £10–15 but you may well be entitled to a free eye check. As a student, you may also be entitled to a voucher towards the cost of spectacles – ask the optician about this.

In England, Scotland and Wales you can currently have free eye checks if you are:

➤ under 16;

➤ under 19 and in full-time education;

➤ getting income support, Jobseeker's Allowance and certain other benefits, depending on income;

➤ are registered blind or partially sighted or need complex lenses;

➤ have diabetes.

There are also a few other conditions which entitle you to free eye tests. Ask your GP or optician.

In Northern Ireland, visit www.adviceguide.org.uk and click the option for Northern Ireland. Navigate to 'Help with health costs'.

If you have a low income, you also may not need to pay or you may have help with buying your spectacles if you need them: if you think this may include you, get a form called HC1 from a local benefit office, NHS hospital, dentist, optician or pharmacist.

How do I find an optician?

Look in your Yellow Pages or at www.yell.com. You do not need to register. Simply walk into or phone an optician's shop and ask for an appointment. You can also use the NHS Equip website, ➡ **Troubleshoot** on page 231.

Stress and happiness

Some of the factors that affect your wellbeing are:

➤ Health – you can't be happy if you are ill. And being unhappy can also make you more vulnerable to illness. Look after your physical health by eating properly, exercising well and treating yourself with kindness and respect.

➤ Money – money can't buy you happiness, as we are always being told. Usually by people who have plenty of it. But there's no doubt that money worries bring stress and unhappiness. ➡ See the **Money** section (pages 11–60) for how to manage your money and where to go for help – and where *not* to go.

➤ Personality – some people do seem to suffer more from stress and unhappiness than others. If you have a negative outlook, it will *seem* very difficult to change it. But actually, you can. You do not have to continue being weighed down by negative thoughts. There are books devoted to helping people change the way they think. Investigate a local library or search on the Internet. If you find the right book for you, it could change your life.

➤ Depression – about 15–20% of adults will suffer from depression. Depression is much more than simply feeling sad and down every now and then – it's a debilitating and crushing illness which stops you being able to function properly. If you feel sad for more than a couple of weeks, do go to your GP. There are lots of things that can help you and your GP is the best starting place.

➤ Work/study – are you in the right job or doing the right course? If not, does this feel temporary or permanent? If temporary, wait for the phase to pass, or change the way you approach your work or study. If permanent, take steps to change it. You do not have to be trapped in the wrong place. Talk to people – friends first. Friends are good at knowing what is right for you, because they know you better than any professional can. Best not to rely on just one friend though – get different views. Even a fantastic friend won't have all the answers.

➤ Social life – are you enjoying the time when you are not working or studying? Do you need to meet some more or different friends? How about taking up a new hobby? Or learning something new and fun or even weird in an evening class? Your local library will have details of courses, classes, groups and social activities you could be involved in.

➤ Stress and anxiety – humans need a bit of stress, otherwise we tend to laze around and eat chocolate all the time. Well, that's what I would do if I didn't have something telling me that if I don't get stuck into my work I won't earn any money and then where would I be? Some people thrive on quite a lot of stress. Others don't. How do you know whether you are suffering from too much stress? Or not dealing with it properly?

• Frequent illness – do you keep getting colds and other minor illnesses? It could be that stress is weakening your immune system.

• Tight chest – do you sometimes feel that something heavy is squashing your chest and you can't take a full breath in? Stress makes us breathe too shallowly and not take in enough oxygen – you need to learn to breathe properly. Put one hand below the bottom of your ribcage. As you breathe in, you should feel your hand being pushed out; if not, you are breathing too much near the top of your lungs and not using them properly. Ask your GP about relaxation techniques or courses.

- Headaches, stomach-aches and nausea are all possible symptoms of a body not dealing with stress.
- Panic attacks – very unfunny episodes where you suddenly think something terrible is going to happen; your breathing becomes fast, you sweat, you are desperate to get out of wherever you are.
- Poor sleep patterns – either taking a long time to get to sleep, or getting to sleep but waking very early and worrying.
- Forgetfulness or making unusual mistakes at work/college – more signs of your brain being overloaded. It can also can be a result of poor sleep.
- Drinking more alcohol than usual, or more than you should – there are lots of reasons why people drink too much and stress is one of them. It is not a good idea and ultimately does absolutely nothing to relieve stress, though it may seem to at the time (➡ page 250).
- Exercise – if you're not getting enough of it, it's not only your body that loses out: it's your mind and mental health too. Exercise is one of the best ways of both preventing and dealing with stress. Even if you don't consider yourself sporty, there are plenty of ways you can get exercise – even if it's going for a brisk walk or a swim, or doing some cycling.

If any of these apply to you, or if you just instinctively know you are under too much stress, whether there's a reason or not, do see your GP. There are so many ways to help, but the problem with stress (and depression and anxiety) is that when you are suffering, you will be the last person to see the solution.

Don't let things get on top of you. Whatever the problem is, there's always someone who can help.

I have another bit of advice too. As that wise old ancient Greek philosopher, Plato, said, 'Know yourself.' Gradually, by noticing the things that get *you* down, the problems that seem too great, by noticing what your body does in negative response – whether it's tensing your shoulders or your jaw or your neck, or becoming irritable, or weepy, or ill – you can best prevent the stress getting on top of you in the first place. Treat yourself well.

Finally, don't spend your spare time with people who get you down, or people who make you feel small and inadequate. Find your kindred spirits, the people you 'click' with, the people you don't have to change yourself for, the people you don't have to perform for and impress.

Finally, finally: laugh. And if nothing seems funny enough to laugh about, find something that is. Preferably with someone else. It's a lot easier to laugh when other people are with you. Laughter is something humans do as part of being sociable and however much you might be one of those people who likes to be alone, everyone feels better after a good laugh with other people. It's like a medicine. In fact, there's something called 'laughter therapy' – a whole load of stressed people sitting around laughing crazily because a medical professional tells them to? Now that's what I call funny.

Troubleshoot

Worried about your health right now? Need immediate reassurance or advice? Not sure if it's an emergency?

➤ In England – Phone NHS Direct – 0845 4647
➤ In Scotland – Phone NHS24 – 08454 242424
➤ In Wales – phone NHS Direct – 0845 4647
➤ In Northern Ireland – phone 0800 665544.

Need answers to a medical question but it's not an emergency? Want to know about an illness? Need to know where to find a doctor or dentist or your nearest Walk-In Injury Clinic?

➤ Visit the NHS Direct website England: www.nhsdirect.nhs.co.uk
➤ Scotland: www.nhs24.co.uk
➤ Wales: www.nhsdirect.wales.nhs.uk
➤ Northern Ireland: www.n-i.nhs.uk

For another excellent (and some might say even better) source of information on all health services and practitioners, *including complementary ones*, visit the Equip website on www.equip.nhs.uk. It's even easier to navigate than the main NHS one: from the home page you can easily jump to sections where you can find any type of practitioner near you, or an A–Z of illnesses or any health topic you can imagine.

For advice about your rights regarding health, including costs and how to access help, visit the impressive website of the Citizens Advice Bureau at www.adviceguide.org.uk. Select either England, Wales, Scotland or Northern Ireland for advice tailored to where you live.

Work and study

Contents

Introduction **235**

Getting work **236**
Your CV 238
Interview tips 239
Can't find work? 240
Temping 240
Starting your own business .
. 241

At work **242**
Your rights 242
Tax and National Insurance . .
. 243
P60 and P45 243

Keeping your job .**244**

Study **245**
Keeping on top of things 245

Troubleshoot **246**

6

WORK AND STUDY

Introduction

Leaving home is not just about how to look after yourself in your new home. There's work – finding it, keeping it and enjoying it. Or there may be college or university, how to cope with the workload as well as perhaps having to earn money to survive. There's your personal safety, your happiness and all the decisions you have to make on your own. Suddenly, the joy of not having teachers and parents telling you what to do all the time may begin to look distinctly tarnished. Suddenly, perhaps you *want* someone to tell you what to do.

Ridiculous. Don't believe a word of it. Life is not actually that difficult. It's just a learning process and each thing you do for the first time is one more item ticked off on life's 'To do' list. You don't need anyone telling you what to do – though you might decide to ask when you *do* want to know something.

In fact, instead of writing *The Leaving Home Survival Guide*, I could just have said, 'Whatever you need to know, ask'. It's the best piece of advice anyone can give. However, I *am* writing *The Leaving Home Survival Guide*, so here's some more advice and information, to save you the trouble of asking everything.

6

WORK AND STUDY

Getting work

Getting work is not easy. However talented, efficient, keen, tidy, positive and downright utterly brilliant you are, you also need luck and perseverance. You have to be prepared for rejection and learn not to take it personally.

But you also have to consider two other things:

➤ Are there some things I am not doing that I could be doing?

➤ Actually, maybe it *is* personal – maybe there's something I'm doing each time I apply and, whatever it is, it's putting potential employers off.

Ask yourself these questions. Most of them are obvious when you think of them:

➤ Am I *selling* myself in my CV, letter and interviews? Am I really showing them how brilliant I am? If not, how can they be expected to know? (➡ **Your CV** on page 238.)

➤ Am I maybe being too arrogant? No one likes arrogance and cockiness. These people have to work with you, for goodness' sake. Quiet confidence is usually the best bet for most jobs.

➤ Is my letter/application form/CV neatly written/typed and presented? Is everything spelt correctly? Get someone to help if you aren't confident about your written language – in fact, get help anyway; someone else might spot something you hadn't noticed.

➤ What do I look like in my interviews? Am I dressed smartly? Is my hair clean and tidy? Do I smell/have bad breath? (Seriously, think about it.) Get your hair cut and wear something a little smarter than you would wear if you were actually working there. For the purposes of an interview, don't think about what *you* want to look like – think about what they want you to look like. If this means removing a piercing, do it.

➤ Do I look directly at the person when they are speaking? (But without staring...) Do I keep looking down/biting my lip/playing with my hair? Ask a friend what habits you have when you are nervous.

➤ Do I sound positive or doubtful about everything? If they ask whether I could do a particular task, do I show lack of confidence or a positive desire to learn? 'I've never done that but I'd be very keen to do it and I know I could if someone gave me some instruction at first,' is a whole lot better than, 'Ooh, er, I don't know about that.'

➤ Am I applying for the right jobs? Do I have the right skills and abilities? Should I perhaps look at something different for now? You may well need to start at a much lower position than you think you are capable of, in order to get started. Once in there, you can show them your brilliance.

➤ Be prepared to have to improve some skills *before* you get the job you want. For example, is your written English letting you down? Can you find someone who can give you a few lessons in apostrophes or whatever? Or take a typing refresher course? Ask at your Jobcentre Plus for training courses available in your area.

Identify places you'd like to work and write to them. Address your letter to the manager if it's a shop/leisure centre, the managing director if it's a small company, or the personnel or 'human resources' director if it's a large company. Make your letter simple, but give a clear outline of who you are and why you would be a fantastic worker for that company. Enclose a copy of your CV. Be flexible about what hours you would be available for – the time to negotiate is when they offer you a job.

Your local Jobcentre Plus can help in many ways. They can help with your CV, too. That's also the place to go if you want and are able to claim benefits, such as Jobseeker's Allowance (which used to be called Unemployment Benefit). You will find your nearest one by looking in the phone book under Jobcentre Plus.

Your CV

CV is short for Curriculum Vitae, which is Latin for 'the course of life'. The purpose is for you to display as clearly as possible all the things you have done and can do. Here are some tips for successful CV writing:

➤ It must be typed and laid out neatly. Ask someone to type it for you if necessary.

➤ Don't lie about anything. You'll regret it.

➤ Start with personal details, such as address and phone number; then list the exams you passed at school or college.

➤ Include other things you have been involved in, such as sport or music, or any hobby – these things all indicate various skills and show you as an interesting person.

➤ List any jobs you have done, in reverse order (i.e. most recent first). Give brief details of your roles in these jobs.

➤ Give details of anything which shows an interest in the job you are applying for. For example, if you are applying for a job in a bookshop, make sure you mention that you are a very keen reader (and then be prepared to talk about this in an interview).

➤ Make your CV relevant to the job you are applying for – so you may need different CVs for different applications. They won't contain very different information, just a different emphasis.

> Take your CV with you to an interview and be prepared to explain more fully any part of it.

> Be prepared to explain any gaps in your employment history – and be honest. The person interviewing you may well have been unemployed at some point too, and will probably be more sympathetic than you imagine. Put a positive spin on it and emphasise how keenly you were looking for work or a positive reason why you were not looking.

> Keep your CV to less than two sides of A4 in length. Do not use both sides of the sheet. Ideally, a CV should be no more than one side.

> Get someone to check it for you before you print it out.

Interview tips

> Research the company before your interview, so you know what they do, where they are based and how large they are. It shows a genuine interest in the company.

> Walk into the room confidently and shake the interviewer's hand firmly – there's nothing like a limp handshake to put someone off. Oh, and wipe your hand before you go in – they don't want firm and sweaty either...

> If more than one person is interviewing you, try to look at each of them in turn, starting with the one who asks the questions.

> Sit comfortably in your chair, not perched on the edge like a nervous sparrow, but don't slouch.

> Don't fidget, fiddle with your hair, bite your fingers or giggle hysterically when they say something mildly amusing.

> At the end (or earlier if appropriate) ask some questions yourself. It's essential to show an interest and not sit there like a boiled potato.

- Be positive and flexible about what you can do or when you could start. Don't be awkward or raise objections, but do be honest if there is something you cannot see your way around.
- One of the hardest things, especially for young people (but older people are often terrible at it too), is managing to seem confident enough but not *too* confident. If you are aware of *trying* to do this, you will be more than half way to achieving it. Looking confident is largely made up of small tricks like looking someone in the eye, speaking slowly, sitting still and comfortably, smiling when possible, and being able to laugh if something goes wrong.
- At the end of the interview, shake hands again and smile as you thank them for their time and look forward to hearing from them. It is a good idea at this point to ask when you might hear from them.

Can't find work?

You will, but while you are looking you could well be eligible for financial help in the benefits system. That's what it's there for. Depending on whether you are able to work or you are already working but your income is very low, and depending on how many hours (if any) you are already working, you may be able to claim Jobseeker's Allowance, Income Support, Housing Benefit or Working Families Tax Credit.

Phone the Benefits Helpline on 0800 882200 (0800 220674 in Northern Ireland) or ask in your local Jobcentre Plus. You will find the address in the phone book.

Temping

Temping is a very good way to get relatively well-paid and very flexible work for short periods of time (though many people do it for a long time). Temping agencies want people with all sorts of skills, though keyboard/computer skills are easily the most in demand nowadays. Go into any job agency or temping agency and see what they have available. They will assess your skills and put you on their files.

Starting your own business

If you have always dreamt of this and have the guts and energy – and an idea – there is no reason why you should not do this. For impartial and expert advice about all the things you need to think about, as well as all the rules about how to do it, contact the national business advice service, Business Link. Either phone 0845 600 9006 or visit the website at www.businesslink.org. They have a free pack to give you, which will cover everything you need to know – except how to have the entrepreneurial idea in the first place...

At work

Your rights

Every employee has certain rights under law. It doesn't matter how long you have worked for your employer or how few hours you do, you still have certain rights. You should also have a contract from your employer, which may give you some extra rights, but cannot give you fewer rights than the law gives you.

> **NOTE:** To have an employee's rights, you need to make sure that you are technically an employee and not self-employed or considered as a freelancer. Sometimes, if you are considered a trainee, you will not have a contract. If you are in any doubt, you should contact your nearest Citizens Advice Bureau (CAB).

Your legal rights and your contract will cover things like:
- health and safety;
- hours of work;
- time off (every employee is entitled to paid holiday, even part-time workers);
- sick pay;
- how much notice you must be given and how much you must give;
- harassment and bullying;
- what your employer is and is not allowed to do.

You have many more rights than this – probably more than you think – and some are quite complicated. You will find excellent, full and free advice either from a Citizens Advice Bureau or on their website at www.adviceguide.org.uk. If you don't think you are being properly treated by your employer, you should also visit the CAB or phone. (You will find the phone number and address of your local one in your phone book.)

Tax and National Insurance

This is dealt with in the money section, ➥ page 42.

P60 and P45

A P60 is a certificate you will be given by your employer at the end of each tax year. (The tax year runs from April 6 to April 5 of the next year). Your P60 tells you how much you have earned and how much tax and NI you have paid. A P45 is a certificate which you are given each time you leave a job. It has details of what you have earned and how much tax and NI you have paid so far that year, and you then give the certificate to your next employer.

Don't worry if you lose your P60 or P45. Your tax office can arrange for you to have another one.

Keeping your job

Some employers are wonderful. Some are not. Some employees are wonderful. Some are not. Whether or not you have a wonderful employer, you will get much more out of life if you are a wonderful employee. Even if you hate your job, you never know when you will meet someone really useful and make a great contact, someone who could perhaps get you a better job. But if you are a rubbish employee, or have been giving that impression, how are you going to get the reference or testimonial that you need for the wonderful job that's going to change your life?

So, how do you make sure you are a wonderful employee?
- ➤ Be punctual. Otherwise you will seriously irritate the people who have to cover for you or who arrive on time.
- ➤ Behave towards others as you would wish them to behave towards you – even if they don't.
- ➤ Ask when you don't understand or are unsure.
- ➤ But use your initiative as well.
- ➤ When you have made a mistake, admit it. Promise to do better next time.
- ➤ Take as little sick leave as possible – again, you just make life harder for everyone.
- ➤ But if you are ill, say so.
- ➤ Dress appropriately and according to the dress code if there is one.
- ➤ Be clean – no body odour or bad breath in the workplace (or anywhere else).
- ➤ Smile.

WORK AND STUDY

Study

Colleges, universities and places of further and higher education have great support systems for students – use them. When you arrive at college or university, you will certainly be told about places like your students' union. The students' union is not only an organization that arranges social events – it is there to ensure that you get the most out of being a student and it has lots of ways to help you with any problem, whether it's to do with health, accommodation, drugs, too much work, or anything else.

Remember the motto: ask. Simple.

Keeping on top of things

Three pieces of advice:

> ➤ Plan ahead – don't leave major pieces of work to the last minute. Why – what's wrong with the last minute? Isn't the last minute as good as any other minute? Ah, but you might be ill in the last minute. Or lose the book you need. Or your computer might decide to have a nervous breakdown and mangle your data. Also, if you've done the work earlier, the last minute is the best time to relax and have fun – while your friends all panic about their mangled data.
> ➤ Ask for help *before* everything gets on top of you. Whether your problems are financial, emotional or work/study-related, there is someone who can help you.
> ➤ Everything passes. What you are worrying about now will soon seem unimportant. Keep things in perspective.

Troubleshoot

Places to help you find work
or deal with issues at work,
including tax:

➤ www.adviceguide.org.uk –
and local Citizens Advice
Bureau offices in your
phone book. Excellent
advice on all aspects of
rights and responsibilities.

➤ www.inlandrevenue.gov.uk
– and local Inland Revenue
Enquiry Centres in your
phone book – all aspects of
tax and National Insurance,
including information
specifically relevant to you.

Keeping yourself safe

7

Contents

Introduction **249**

Alcohol **250**
Working out units 251
Minimizing the effects of
    alcohol 252
Getting home safely 252

Drugs **254**
Drug rape 254

**Avoiding being
a victim of crime** .**257**
If you are a victim of crime . .
. 258

Travelling abroad .**260**
Passport 261
Visas 261

Troubleshoot **262**

Introduction

You may have left home, but your parents are still worried about your safety. Parents can be quite irritating about things like that. Funny how they care so much – you'd think they could stop fussing now that you're big enough and ugly enough to look after yourself. I can't promise that they'll stop worrying just because they know you have *The Leaving Home Survival Guide* but I can hope. And you can only read – and *be careful*.

Taking calculated risks is an important part of living. Taking foolish ones can be part of dying.

Alcohol

Drinking too much can make you take bad decisions and not even realize they are bad. By bad I mean dangerous. When you are even moderately drunk, you are more likely to:

> ➤ have unprotected sex;
> ➤ have sex which you later regret;
> ➤ say yes to something you would not normally say yes to;
> ➤ allow someone to spike your drink;
> ➤ take other risks, such as getting into a car with a driver who has been drinking, getting into a car with a stranger or deciding to walk home alone;
> ➤ have an accident, such as crossing a road and being knocked over, falling out of a window or into water;
> ➤ not notice how cold you are and suffer hypothermia.

How do you avoid or minimize these risks? Well, obviously, you could choose not to drink too much, but it's not up to me to tell you that. You can make your own decisions. But the risks of drinking too much don't stop with accidents. There's the risk to your health as well, particularly the likelihood of brain damage that can't be reversed or repaired – each time you get drunk you lose a whole load more brain cells. Your memory and ability to recall information will be damaged too. Unfortunately, that's permanent.

However, if this is how you choose to spend your money and brain cells, at least make sure you stick with your friends. Never go home on your own. When you go out, make an agreement with your friends that you will not split up. With any luck, at least one of you will stay sober enough to prevent tragedy.

If a friend is very drunk, you deciding not to drink any more and look after her or him could save your friend's life. If someone becomes unconscious and cannot be roused, you should call an ambulance immediately. Put the person in the recovery position (➡ page 309) and keep him/her warm while waiting for the ambulance.

Long-term alcohol problems are something to watch out for, too. The government recommends that men should drink a maximum of twenty-one units of alcohol in one week, preferably spread out over the week. Women should drink no more than fourteen units. But do you know what a unit is?

It's not as simple as saying 'one glass of wine' or 'half a pint of beer'. What's a glass? How strong is the beer? Is it dry wine or sweet? How much vodka? What about cocktails or things like alcopops?

Working out units

A bottle or can will have a percentage figure on it. This percentage relates to ABV – alcohol by volume. (The old-fashioned term was 'proof', but this actually describes a different way of measuring alcohol.) Supposing a beer, for example, is 5% ABV, that means that there are five units of alcohol in one litre of that particular drink. So, if a beer was 5%, one pint (roughly half a litre) would actually be two and a half units.

The same applies to wine. A weak wine, such as a sweetish wine, might be 10% ABV. A bottle is 70 cl of wine. So if you drank a bottle of it, you would be drinking seven units. However, much of the wine that we drink nowadays in this country is stronger than 10%, often 13–14%. So, if you drank a bottle, (which comes to about six small glasses), that would be nearly ten units and one reasonable glass would take you near the two units mark.

With spirits, such as vodka, a unit is usually one *small* pub measure. A double vodka or double 'shot' is two units. But when it's mixed in a cocktail, you really haven't a clue how much you are drinking. That's the real danger – you are suddenly not in control of what you are drinking.

> **WARNING:** Every young person nowadays knows this, but don't forget it: never leave your drink unattended. Take it with you wherever you go or leave it with a friend – but not a drunk friend. If you think your drink might have been spiked, chuck it away – and tell someone (➡ pages 254–6).

Minimizing the effects of alcohol

➤ Drink plenty of water – ideally alternate an alcoholic drink with a glass of water or a soft drink.

➤ Spread your drinking out over a long evening.

➤ Don't drink on an empty stomach.

Getting home safely

➤ Carry a phone number for a taxi company that you know. Better still – pre-book. Then you know the taxi will come and you won't be waiting on the street.

➤ When you go out, put enough money for a taxi fare somewhere separate from the rest of your money – and don't spend it on anything else.

➤ Never let someone drive when you know they've had more than one small drink – and don't drive yourself. Never assume that because you think you can walk in a straight line you can drive. You risk death – or killing someone else.

➤ Avoid walking at night on your own. But if it's unavoidable: stick to the brightest streets; carry your keys in your hand; keep your money and phone in a separate place from your handbag/wallet; never have your address together with your keys; and walk strongly, as though you are not afraid.

➤ If you are mugged, scream loudly but do not try to hold onto your bag or phone – give them up.

➤ Leave a light on at home, so you can get in the house easily.

➤ If you find signs of forced entry, do not go into the house on your own.

Drugs

If you take illegal drugs, there are no ways in which I can advise you to do this safely. It is against the law (including taking cannabis) and risky for health reasons too. If you want to look after yourself, don't take illegal substances or abuse solvents. I've said my piece.

If you do take something, make sure you understand the health implications of that particular drug first, as well as how to recognize danger signs. A good source of information for young people is TheSite website at www.thesite.org. Click on 'Drink & Drugs'.

If someone you are with becomes ill and you know or suspect that the person has taken a drug, call an ambulance and tell the ambulance staff what you suspect. What's more frightening – getting yourself or your friend into trouble or someone dying?

Drug rape

Drug rape is the term used to describe someone spiking your drink (usually) so that you are unable to resist while they rape you. It is impossible to know how frequent this crime is, but it is very definitely something you need to be aware of and protect yourself from as much as possible. It is sometimes called date rape.

The most well-known drugs used in this callous and disgraceful crime are Rohypnol and GHB. However, alcohol on its own could create the same result – certainly you are more likely to have non-consensual sex if you are out of it on alcohol. Victims of drug rape, however, do describe their experiences as being quite different from simply being too drunk.

It is also possible to be offered a spiked cigarette.

Although rape victims are more often female, rape does also happen to men, so men need to be equally aware of the risk of drug rape.

Here are some unpleasant facts:

➤ Around 780 men and women in the UK have reported being drugged and raped.

➤ The number of reported cases of drug rape is rising by 50% each month.

➤ There are 40 different drugs which are known to have been used in date rape cases.

➤ 70% of drug rapes are carried out by someone the victim knows.

➤ Only 12 hours after being taken, GHB cannot be detected.

➤ Only 48 hours after being taken, Rohypnol cannot be detected.

➤ There has been a 400% increase in recorded cases of date rape over the past decade.

Scientists are working on a simple test with which you can test a drink to see if has been spiked. Reports indicate that these testing sticks could be available within a year or so.

Until then, prevention is your only form of attack:

➤ At the start of your evening, tell friends where you are going.

➤ Stay with a friend if at all possible and arrange with each other how you are going to go home; arrange that if one of you goes home with someone else, the other will notice who you have gone with.

➤ A good friend should notice if you are behaving strangely – discuss strategies and possibilities with your friends in advance.

➤ Do not leave your drink unattended.

➤ Keep your hand over your glass/bottle.

➤ If you feel odd, tell your friends immediately; if you are not with friends, tell the barman or bouncers, or as many people as possible.

If you wake up next morning and think someone has had sex with you while you were asleep or you have memories of feeling strangely not in control of your thoughts and actions, get help immediately. The drugs may take your memory away completely, so if you wake up and don't know how you got to bed (whether it's your own bed or not), and there are signs that you have had sex – underwear scattered around, sore genitals, any bruising, anything suspicious at all – you may have been raped.

These drugs typically leave the body quickly so take the following steps:

➤ Do not go to the toilet, if possible.
➤ Do not wash yourself.
➤ Call the police or go to a police station (with a friend).
➤ Insist on a urine and blood sample being taken immediately.

You will *not* be prosecuted for taking drugs, even if you knew you were taking a drug.

Even if you think you are too late to do anything, still report it to the police. Also, I am afraid you will need to visit your GP – it is impossible to rule out the possibility that you contracted a sexually transmitted disease, or even HIV. The latter is unlikely, but it is important that you know, for all sorts of reasons.

For further advice about any aspect of drug rape, contact the Roofie Foundation. They have a 24 hour helpline: 0800 783 2980 and a website at www.roofie.com.

> **REMEMBER:** All the above advice applies to men and women equally.

Avoiding being a victim of crime

A survey of university and college students conducted in 2003 showed that 33% had been victims of crime in the last year. Most of this was burglary or theft. (Burglary is when a burglar enters your home; theft is when the stealing does not involve entering your home.)

Some tips:
- Lock doors even when you are in. Install a spy-hole so you can see who is there before opening the door.
- Lock all doors and windows at night and every time you go out, even for a few minutes. Half of all crimes happen without planning – a dishonest person just happens to see an open window and snatches whatever can be seen. And remember to check the terms of your insurance policy (➡ page 46).
- Never leave anything in your car – even an old coat is tempting to a thief, who might think there is a wallet in it.
- Don't show off your money or your phone.
- Always stay in a group of friends, if possible.
- If you are on your own, never stop to give directions or answer a question, unless there are lots of people around.
- Consider carrying a security alarm. Many universities provide these free. You could also ask at a police station or order from the Internet. They typically cost around £5.
- At night, have your mobile phone by your bed. And keep your handbag, wallet, etc. by you too.

➤ Be careful when you get cash from a cash machine. Don't let anyone see the number you put in. Be very suspicious if someone tries to help you when your card gets stuck – there is a scam that works on this principle. Keep your wits about you and do not flash your money around.

➤ Strongly consider going to self-defence classes. This is not the same as martial arts, such as judo, and you will not learn to smash three bricks with the side of your hand. This is about all the many strategies you can use to keep yourself safe. If a group of you get together, the police will often create a course especially for your group.

Don't wait for a crime to happen before getting advice. Your local police station will have a Crime Prevention Officer and they will be more than happy to advise you. They will be able to tell you how to get the best locks, for example. Look in the phone book under 'Police' and find the station nearest to you.

If you are a student or on a course of any sort, your place of learning will almost certainly provide safety advice and anti-crime packages, including things like special pens to mark your property, and special advice relevant to your town or area. Use this advice and keep the information by your phone at home.

If you are a victim of crime

➤ Scream – loud and long. Keep screaming till someone helps you.

➤ If you lose a bank or credit card, phone your bank to cancel it as soon as you notice. Keep the number by your phone so that you can do this. ➡ **Card protection and fraud** section on page 33 for more details.

➤ Report any crime committed against you, even if you think there's no point. The police need to know. Even if they can't find your stolen property, it helps them to know where to target their efforts and resources.

➤ If it's not an emergency – in other words, if the crime has already happened and there is no further danger – phone your local police station, not 999. However, if you think the criminal could still be nearby and you are frightened, *do* dial 999.

➤ You may feel shocked afterwards. When intruders come into your home it is particularly horrible. The idea that a stranger has been looking through your things, even if they haven't stolen anything very precious, is a really awful feeling. People talk about feeling violated. Talk to someone – Victim Support will help you. The police will tell you how to get in touch with them, or you can visit their website (www.victimsupport.org.uk) to find a local office.

➤ There will probably be things you can do to make yourself and your home safer. The police can send a Crime Prevention Officer to advise you. This costs nothing and the police are happy to do it.

➤ If you are a victim of rape, call the police immediately – they need to do tests which can make a difference to whether your rapist is convicted or not. You will be seen by a female officer with special training in helping victims of rape. If you are a victim of homosexual rape, the police have been trained in dealing with this, too. For more details about date rape, ➡ pages 254–6.

Never make a fake 999 call. It is a criminal offence. Apart from that, imagine if your fake call-out stopped one of your friends getting an ambulance or whatever help was needed.

➡ page 45 for information about insuring your possessions – this means that if you are burgled, you will be able to buy replacements. Insurance can also cover some things that you carry around with you as well. Check it out.

Travelling abroad

Going on holiday with friends is a big part of leaving home and being independent. Travelling abroad is exciting at any age but, without the responsibilities of having your own children, now is a fantastic time to do it. But different countries have different systems and, just when you are learning how your own country's laws and systems work, you'll need to cope with a different culture. And respect it.

People in different countries may also have different views about acceptable behaviour. It's important to find out what is OK and what is not in the country you plan to visit. Alcohol laws vary, for example.

Tourists are very vulnerable to crime. Criminals know that if you are a stranger in the country, and relaxing on holiday, you are less able to look after yourself. You may be more interested in your suntan development than watching your back pocket. You need to be more, not less, careful on holiday and to find out before you go if there are any special risks in the place you are visiting. These publications are extremely useful:

➤ *Staying Safe Away From Home* is a booklet costing 40p, available from the Suzy Lamplugh Trust. ➡
  Troubleshoot on page 262 for the website or phone number.
➤ *Your Passport to Safer Travel* by Mark Hodson is a book published by Thomas Cook Publishing, covering 200 countries and all the various things you need to consider to enjoy your holiday and not become a victim. It costs £6.99 and is also available from the Suzy Lamplugh Trust.
➤ *Rough Guide: First Time Around the World* by Doug Lansky.

Do plenty of research about your destination before you go: you will get much more out of your trip if you know what there is to do, what to take, what to buy and generally what to expect. Guidebooks can be expensive but you can get free information from the tourist board of the country you are visiting – details will be on the Internet or in a library.

If you are going to a country within the European Community, you need to get an E111 from the post office. Take it abroad with you – it gives you access to free medical care. But you will still need insurance to cover other things. For example, if you break a leg or get appendicitis, being flown home with such medical conditions can cost thousands of pounds.

Passport

If you haven't already got a passport, get a form from your post office. And be prepared for a lengthy session working out what all the questions mean. Allow several weeks for your passport to arrive.

Don't try travelling on a passport that only has a few months left on it – you may well not be allowed to travel, even if you plan to return well within the time.

Visas

As well as a passport, you may need something called a visa. This depends on what sort of passport you have and which country you are visiting. A travel agent will be able to tell you if you need one and how to get it. Do this several weeks before you plan to travel. The UK government website www.ukpa.gov.uk also has all the information you need.

If you have an EU passport, you will not need a visa to travel to another EU country.

KEEPING YOURSELF SAFE

Troubleshoot

Who to turn to for general help

➤ The Samaritans – helpline for anyone feeling depressed or suicidal – 08457 90 90 90
➤ Your Students' Union representative if you are at university or college.
➤ Your GP.

Lots of places to find out more about keeping yourself safe

➤ www.good2bsecure.co.uk – crime prevention advice aimed at students.
➤ www.crimestoppers-uk.org or 0800 555 111 – for people who have information about a crime. You can report it without giving your name. You will be helping to prevent crime and protect decent people.
➤ www.victimsupport.org.uk – if you have been a victim of any crime, they can give you advice about preventing it again and about dealing with any fears you now have.
➤ www.nusonline.co.uk – the union of students website.
➤ www.rapecrisis.co.uk or 0115 9003560 (England and Wales) 0131 556 9737 (Scotland) – every type of help for anyone who has been raped.
➤ www.roofie.com – the Roofie Foundation, the only organization dedicated entirely to the issue of drug-rape.
➤ www.suzylamplugh.org or 020 8392 1839 – advice about personal safety.
➤ Your local police station – write the number at the back of this book.

The law and you

Contents

Introduction 265

Alcohol and the law . . .
. . . . 266

Drugs and the law 267
Class A, B or C? 267
Cannabis 267

Cars and the law 269
A car accident 269

Tenants and the law
. . . . 270

Customers and the law
. . . . 271
If you are not happy with
something you buy . . . 271
How long do you have to
complain? 272
Cooling-off period 273
Disagreements with a
shop/company 274
Exceptions/problems . . . 274
Caveat emptor 274
Read the small print 274
Delivered goods 275

Noisy neighbours and
other annoyances
. . . . 276

Being arrested . . . 277

Troubleshoot 279

8

THE LAW AND YOU

Introduction

Most people want to stay on the right side of the law. I highly recommend it. After all, do you really want to lie awake at night waiting for your door to be smashed down in a dawn raid? Or to feel you have to leap into a darkened doorway every time you see a police car cruising around? Or to break out in a sweat every time you hear a distant siren?

Also, the law isn't only for telling you what you can't do. It also tells other people, or companies, what they can't do to you. It's important to know what you can't do, but it's also very empowering if you know what people can't do to you. This chapter tries to point you in the right direction for both those things.

However, laws change. There are also some differences between the legal system in Scotland and the rest of the UK. Finally, there can be exceptions and complicated clauses. If it was too simple, there'd be nothing for lawyers to do. So this chapter can only make quite general points, and can't really help you in very complicated situations. If you are unsure of your rights on a particular issue, you should contact your local Citizens Advice Bureau.

Alcohol and the law

In the UK you can buy alcohol once you are 18. Everyone knows that. In some other countries, and particularly many states in the US, you have to be 21. Once you are 18 or over, the law says:

➤ You must not drive while under the influence of alcohol. What is 'under the influence'? You may think you are completely sober, but if you have more than a certain amount of alcohol in your blood, you will be charged with drink-driving. Even if you have not caused an accident. The penalties are very severe and include prison. Worse, you may kill someone or yourself. How do you know when you are over the limit? You don't, so don't risk it. The only way to be completely sure is not to drive if you have had any alcohol. One small glass of wine or half a pint of beer *may* have been processed out of your body after one hour or more, but many people do not get rid of alcohol so quickly, and several drinks mount up. Don't drink and drive.

➤ You must not be 'drunk and disorderly'. If your being drunk causes a disturbance or a problem for other people, you can be arrested.

➤ You could also be charged with 'being drunk in charge of a bicycle' for example.

If you are going to drink, don't annoy other people or cause danger to yourself or others, or you will find yourself on the wrong side of the law.

Drugs and the law

Under the Misuse of Drugs Act it is an offence to:
- ➤ possess a controlled substance unlawfully;
- ➤ possess a controlled substance with intent to supply it;
- ➤ supply a controlled drug;
- ➤ allow your place of work/living to be used for drug taking.

A 'controlled substance' may also be a prescription drug – it is illegal to possess a prescription drug if you do not have a prescription for it. Certain tranquillizers, for example, such as valium, or vicodin, would come into this category. Nowadays, many drugs like this are traded over the Internet – remember that if it is a prescription-only drug you are breaking the law if you do not have a prescription. They are dangerous medicines if not used in a controlled way and prescribed by a doctor who understands your medical circumstances.

Class A, B or C?

The law views drugs as belonging to different categories, or 'classes'. Heroin, for example, is Class A (regarded as the most serious class) and valium is Class C. All of them are illegal – it is only the penalties that are different.

Cannabis

(Also called marijuana/pot/weed/hash/dope.)
Cannabis gets a special mention here because of the confusion after it was downgraded from Class B to Class C in January

2004. IT IS STILL ILLEGAL in exactly the same way as it was before. You are still not allowed to possess, grow or supply it, or allow your home/place of work to be used for taking it. The only thing that has changed is the maximum possible penalty – you can still go to prison, but the maximum term for possession is two years rather than five. But note that the penalty for supplying/dealing all Class C drugs has *increased* from five to fourteen years.

Supplying includes giving it to a friend.

In practice, as an adult caught in possession of a Class C drug, you would be most likely to have a warning and have the drug confiscated. But if there were 'aggravating factors' (such as smoking it in public, behaving dangerously or offending several times despite warnings) you could well be arrested and prosecuted. And you could go to prison.

The laws surrounding drug misuse and the classification of drugs are under review and may change quickly. There's an old saying, 'ignorance is no defence' – and it's true, because not knowing what the law is will not help you in court.

Cars and the law

Obviously, you have to obey the rules of the Highway Code. The other aspects of the law which affect you and your car are:

➤ You must not drive when unfit to do so, for example, after taking alcohol or drugs, or when drowsy for any reason (some medicines make you sleepy; so do late nights in clubs).

➤ You must not use a mobile phone while driving (even if stationary at a traffic light). You also must not do anything else which spoils your concentration – people have been prosecuted for dangerous driving when eating a sandwich or drinking from a water bottle.

➤ You must have an up-to-date tax disc and you must display it. If your car is not being driven at all and is not kept on a public road, you must inform the DVLA (0870 850 4444) to apply for exemption. Details are on www.direct.gov.uk.

➤ You must have up-to-date 'third party insurance'.

➤ You must not allow your car to be used for criminal activity.

A car accident

The Highway Code is very clear about your first duty in the event of an accident (whether you are involved or not). I discovered this, to my eternal irritation, during my own driving test. This was how the conversation went – it is etched on my memory:

Tester: What is the first thing you should do in the event of an accident?

Me: Call the police?

Tester: What is the first thing you should do in the event of
        an accident?

Me: Try to help anyone who is injured?

Tester: What is the first thing you should do in the event of
        an accident?

Me: Er, scream? Have a panic attack? Do some yoga?

Tester: I am prohibited from expressing this question in any
        other way. What is the first thing you should do in
        the event of an accident?

Me: Oh go on, I give up.

Tester: The first thing you should do in the event of an
        accident is to stop.

Me: (silently grinding teeth) Ahhh.

Yes, you should stop. If you haven't already. Seriously, the
point is that if you are a witness to an accident, however small,
and whether or not you were involved in it, you should first
stop your car safely. Obviously, you should not put yourself in
danger. If you are frightened or suspicious, you should drive on
a little way and then call the police. Oh, but stop before calling
them. Of course. I know that now.

Tenants and the law

For your rights and responsibilities as a tenant, ➡ pages 73–5.

Customers and the law

Your rights as a customer are not simple. The Citizens Advice Bureau website has excellent information on the details of consumer law and if your situation does not fit with anything listed below, contact them.

Put simply, anything you buy must be:

➤ **'Of satisfactory quality'**. In other words, it should be of the standard that a 'reasonable person' would expect, judging from the price, description and packaging. You can also object to the appearance, even if the item works perfectly well.

➤ **'Fit for the purpose'**. In other words the item must do what you would normally expect from such an item.

➤ **'Match its description'**. In other words, if there was a description of the goods, it must be accurate, even if it was only an oral description.

If you are not happy with something you buy

➤ Examine and try it as soon as you get it home. If you keep it for a long time and then take it back to the shop, they may refuse to give you a refund (though there is no law that says how long 'a long time' is).

➤ If you can't get back to the shop soon, phone them and explain the problem.

➤ If there is something wrong with it (under the three rules above), you have the right to demand a refund or a replacement – whichever you prefer. You do *not* have to accept a credit note. You do not have to have the item repaired. If it's new, you should be given a new one or a refund.

➤ If there's nothing wrong with it but you just don't like it or you changed your mind, the shop does not have to take it back. Some do. Some will offer you a refund – this is more than the law tells them to do.

➤ Check the company's policy on refunds. They may have a more generous policy than the law demands. They will not have a less generous policy. That's what it means when it says 'This does not affect your statutory rights' – your statutory rights are the ones the law gives you. They can't be taken away.

➤ If you bought the item with a credit card, the credit card company has a duty to help you, jointly with the company you bought the item from (if it cost more than £100). Some credit cards, such as American Express and Diners Club are not covered by the Consumer Credit Act and therefore are not obliged to help you. For details of what to do, see www.bbc.co.uk/watchdog/guides_to/credit/index4.shtml or contact the Citizens Advice Bureau.

➤ Keep your receipt safe – it's the only way you can prove from whom you bought the item and when you bought it.

➤ Very important point: your argument is with the shop or company who sold the item to you, *not* the manufacturer. The shop can get its own refund from the manufacturer but *must* give you your statutory rights. Very often, a shop will say you should use the manufacturer's guarantee – *you do not have to do this.*

How long do you have to complain?

Some items have a fixed guarantee. For electrical items, this is usually one year. For mobile phones and a few other things, it may be three months. For other items, there is no fixed period.

If something breaks or goes wrong after the period of guarantee, or if there was no period of guarantee, the rule would be what a 'reasonable person' might feel was an appropriate amount of time. If, for example, a pair of shoes fell to pieces after four or five months, I would say that was not acceptable. And I am a very reasonable person. If they fell to pieces after a year, I'd say that was not brilliant, but not unacceptable. Anything between that, it would depend on things like how expensive they were, how much I had worn them, whether I had gone hill-walking in them (unlikely, knowing me) and what sort of mood I was in. You see that the 'reasonable person' definition is a bit tricky.

Cooling-off period

A shop may give you a period of time in which you can change your mind – usually 28 days. They do not have to.

However, many types of purchase that are made *away from a shop* (such as over the phone or via the Internet or by someone calling at your door) have a legal 'cooling-off period'. During this time you can cancel without penalty, and get a full refund. Never buy something in this way without knowing what the cooling-off period is.

My personal advice would be never buy anything from someone who turns up unannounced on your doorstep. I always say to these people that if they have something worth selling they can give or send me a leaflet.

Note: if a doorstep trader does not tell you about the cooling-off period and your right to cancel, the contract is illegal and you do not have to pay. Take any problems of this sort to your local Trading Standards Office.

Never ever buy anything from anyone if you don't have contact details for them.

Disagreements with a shop/company

➤ Ask to speak to the manager.

➤ Say that you believe your rights as a consumer are being violated and that you are going to contact the Citizens Advice Bureau (or, if you think they are wrongly describing something or selling inferior goods, Trading Standards).

➤ If it was bought with a credit card, contact your credit card company.

Exceptions/problems

You will not be entitled to a refund or replacement if:

➤ the fault was pointed out to you at the time – for example, a sale item was marked as 'soiled';

➤ you have damaged the goods yourself by using them incorrectly;

➤ you have tried to repair the item yourself.

Different rules also apply if you bought the goods:

➤ from an individual, not a company;

➤ at an auction.

Caveat emptor

This is Latin for 'let the buyer beware'. I knew all those years of learning Latin verbs were going to come in useful one day. What it means nowadays is that you must take every reasonable precaution not to be ripped off. But there are plenty of laws there to support you when your carefulness fails or something goes wrong.

Read the small print

Really a part of *caveat emptor*. Take your time to read guarantees properly. Don't sign anything unless you are sure you understand. Don't sign before reading – this sounds a bit obvious, but actually it's very difficult when some eager salesperson is hovering over you and a queue is building up behind you. Do not let yourself be rushed.

Delivered goods

If something is delivered to you, perhaps from a mail order company, you have exactly the same rights as if you bought from a shop. More, in fact, because mail order companies know that you can't always tell from a catalogue what something looks like, so they will let you try before you buy. They will usually also pay your postage if you have to return something.

If something is actually faulty, they *must* pay your postage. Don't post it back and then claim a refund – phone and ask them to collect it or to send you a sticker for the package, so you don't have to pay postage at all.

Noisy neighbours and other annoyances

Excess noise might concern you in two ways: either your noise annoys someone else or someone else's noise annoys you. There's no doubt, noise annoys. It can also be extremely stressful for the person annoyed by the noise. And that's where the law comes in. The law is at the same time clear and vague. Laws are clever like that. Basically, no one is allowed to annoy anyone else with their noise or any other aspect of behaviour.

That's clear. And vague. Vague because who decides what is a loud enough noise or annoying enough habit to be stopped? The clear answer is: your local council.

So, what should you do if you are fed up with your neighbours' behaviour?

➤ If possible, speak to them in a friendly way. They may simply not realize they are disturbing you. If you sound reasonable, they are more likely to be reasonable. But life's not always so simple...

➤ If the problem is happening now (such as a loud party after 11 o'clock at night), call the police. You do not have to give your name.

➤ If the problem is not happening now, contact your local council. If you are a council tenant, contact the housing department. If you are not, contact the environmental health department. These numbers will be in the phone book under 'council'.

The council will take it seriously and investigate. They may ask you to keep a diary. It helps if any other affected neighbours do the same. The council may want to come and witness the noise.

You have a right to enjoy your own home, whether you are a tenant or a home owner.

Being arrested

As soon as you are arrested, you *must* be told what you are being arrested for. You will be taken to a police station. Do not try to resist arrest – it is a crime, even if you know you haven't done anything. And if you have done something, resisting arrest will make it worse.

At the police station:

➤ You must be allowed to see a duty solicitor and you will not have to pay (unless you have and want to use your own solicitor).

➤ If you want someone to know where you are, the police must arrange this.

➤ You must be allowed to read a copy of the Codes of Practice and your rights must be explained.

➤ While being questioned, you must be given adequate food and drink and toilet breaks. You must not be kept in discomfort or pressurized unfairly.

➤ You do have to give your name and address.

➤ You do not have to answer any other question – though if you do not, and if you are charged and your case goes to court, the court will be told that you did not answer. Wait till the solicitor arrives and follow his/her advice.

➤ The interview will probably be taped. If not, notes may be taken – you must be shown these notes and sign them if you think they are a fair version of what was said.

➤ You cannot *usually* be held for more than 24 hours without charge.

➤ The police may take your fingerprints.

➤ They may also photograph you – but they cannot force you to be photographed.

➤ The fingerprints and photo must be destroyed if you are not charged, or if you are found not guilty.

You may be charged, bailed or cautioned – your solicitor will explain all of these.

From the moment you are arrested, you will make things better for yourself if you are not aggressive or violent. Co-operate with your solicitor and any help you are given. The police are simply not allowed to ride over your rights – and if they do, the case against you will be weakened by any mistreatment of you. It's right to stand up for your rights, but you should rely on your solicitor to fight your corner for you.

If you later feel that your solicitor did not do a good job for you or you feel unhappy about what happened, ask your Citizens Advice Bureau for their view.

There's a well-known saying: the law is an ass. Everyone has stories about utterly bizarre laws. However, odd as it may seem when you are on the wrong side of it, a law is there for the purpose of helping and strengthening society as a whole. It's there to protect the vulnerable, the victim, against the violent, the villain. And to allow law-abiding citizens to live in peace.

It works pretty well most of the time. For an ass. Just keep your eyes open and stay on the right side of it – and you'll find you hardly notice it's there.

Oh, and remember: what should you do in the event of an accident? STOP.

Troubleshoot

➤ TheSite – that completely
  brilliant website for young
  people that I can't help
  mentioning.
  www.thesite.org

➤ Citizens Advice Bureau –
  look in your phone book
  for your local office or see
  www.adviceguide.org.uk.

➤ Directgov – the very useful
  government website.
  www.direct.gov.uk

EMERGENCIES

How to use the emergency section

Don't wait for an emergency before reading this section. Reading through every part now will give you advantages when an emergency actually happens – it could even mean you'll save a life.

> ➤ The stress of being in a real life and death situation can make you panic and be less able to understand brand-new information.
> ➤ You'll know what emergencies are covered in this book.
> ➤ You'll know where the information is when you really need it.
> ➤ Although you will probably forget some of the information in the heat of the moment, it will at least feel familiar.
> ➤ You will be able to react more quickly.

Practise the ABC and CPR techniques on pages 306–8. You may feel silly practising the kiss of life on a pillow, but it could make all the difference to your ability to stay cool when an emergency actually happens. And you could save the life of a friend.

Index of emergency pages

The emergencies come in alphabetical order, with medical ones before others.

Medical emergencies 287

Asthma attack/breathing difficulties 288

Bleeding 289

Burns 290

Choking 291

Diabetic emergency 294

Electric shock 295

Epileptic fit 296

Fractures/dislocation 297

Head injury 298

Heart attack 299

Meningitis 300

Nosebleed 302

Poisoning 303

Shock 305

Unconsciousness and CPR 306

Recovery position 309

Other emergencies 311

Burglary/crime 312

Car accident 313

Fire 316

Gas 318

Homelessness 319

Loss of wallet/handbag/credit cards 320

Water leak 322

Medical emergencies

NOTE: When an emergency requires hospital treatment, decide the fastest and safest way to get the patient there. Dial 999 for an ambulance if that is the quickest way. But sometimes it may be quicker to drive the patient yourself – do this, but only if this IS safer and quicker.

If you call an ambulance, medical treatment can begin as soon as the ambulance arrives. The paramedics or ambulance personnel will have life-saving equipment. This is another reason why dialling 999 may often be the right thing to do. If it isn't, the operator will advise you.

If in doubt, dial 999 –

they will tell you what to do.

Asthma attack/ breathing difficulties

Panic makes breathing difficulties worse because a panicking patient needs more oxygen. **The most important thing is to try to keep the sufferer calm.**

Other steps

➤ Get the casualty to sit down, leaning slightly forward with the elbows supported on a table or something else solid.

➤ Open windows to ensure the person gets as much fresh air as possible (though very cold air will make asthma worse, so avoid this).

➤ Get the casualty to take prescribed medication if available. The patient should use the inhaler as much as necessary – overdose is not an issue.

999 If the symptoms do not improve quickly, dial 999 as an emergency.

NOTE: A steamy environment can help in a mild attack – close the bathroom door and window; turn hot water taps on and fill the bath/basin and/or run a hot shower to create a steamy atmosphere.

Bleeding

➤ Press a clean pad firmly on the wound for up to 20 minutes. If there is an object in the wound, such as glass, press beside the wound instead (on the side nearer the heart).

➤ Raise the injured part of the body and support it whilst maintaining pressure (but not if there is injury to the bone, such as a fracture or dislocation).

➤ If bleeding continues or is impossible to control, press firmly on the artery above the wound (in whichever direction is nearer the heart), but this can be dangerous and should only be done if there is no alternative.

➤ Treat as for shock ➡ page 305.

999 Dial 999:

➤ if the bleeding does not stop or is particularly fast. If in doubt, do dial 999.

➤ if a part of the body, such as a finger, has been severed. Wrap it in a bag or clingfilm and place it in ice – but don't let the body part touch the ice directly. Send the severed part with the casualty to hospital.

➤ if the bleeding stops but blood loss has been significant.

Burns

Treat as an emergency any burn that:
- ➤ is larger than half the patient's hand;
- ➤ has broken or blistered the skin;
- ➤ is on the face, head or fingers.

For small burns, ➡ page 223.

999 **For a severe burn**
- ➤ A severe burn needs hospital treatment. Drive the patient to hospital, or, if this is not possible or if the patient is feeling unwell, dial 999. The patient is likely to be suffering shock, which can be dangerous.
- ➤ While waiting, or before driving the patient to hospital, run cold water over the area for 10–20 minutes, if possible.
- ➤ Cover the burnt area with clingfilm. If none is available, cover loosely with a clean, non-fluffy cloth, such as a clean tea towel.
- ➤ Keep the patient lying down, warm and calm.
- ➤ Treat for shock (➡ page 305).
- ➤ Do not give the patient anything to eat or drink.
- ➤ Do not interfere with the wound, for example, by puncturing a blister.
- ➤ Remove tight clothing or jewellery, as the area will swell.

Choking

If the person is able to cough, the airway is not blocked – allow the patient's natural coughing reflexes to take over. However, if the symptoms worsen or turn into the following signs, treat it as an emergency.

Signs

➤ Difficulty in speaking and breathing.
➤ Blueness around lips and skin.
➤ Patient pointing at or clutching the throat.

IMPORTANT: Do not use fingers to feel down the throat without looking, as the obstruction may become worse.

Treatment

The technique depends on the age:

1. Baby (under one year old)
2. Child
3. Adult
4. Unconscious adult

1. Baby (under one year old)

➤ Place the baby face down along your forearm and give five sharp slaps across the back.
➤ If this fails, turn the baby onto its back and place on your lap.
➤ Give five sharp thrusts on the lower breast bone (*not* the abdomen) with two fingers only.

- ➤ Check the airway and remove the foreign body if you can see it.
- ➤ If unsuccessful, repeat the process.

2. Young child (up to around 5 or 6, depending on size)

- ➤ Place the child face down on your lap and give five sharp slaps between the shoulder blades.
- ➤ If this fails, turn the child onto his/her back and lay on your lap.
- ➤ Using one hand give five sharp thrusts to the lower breast bone.
- ➤ Check the mouth and remove any foreign body you can see.
- ➤ If choking persists, give five firm upward thrusts to the central upper abdomen. Repeat the cycle.

3. Adult and older child

- ➤ Stand behind the standing casualty and give five sharp slaps between the shoulder blades.
- ➤ If this fails, perform the 'Heimlich manoeuvre' (abdominal thrusts). To do this:
  - • Stand behind the standing casualty.
  - • Place your hands around and in front of the casualty.
  - • Make a fist with one hand and place the other hand around the fist.
  - • Rest your fist just below the breast bone.
  - • Pull sharply inwards and upwards to the upper part of the abdomen, with both hands.
  - • Repeat the abdominal thrusts three or four times. Continue the five back slaps and three or four abdominal thrusts alternately.

4. Unconscious adult

- ➤ Check the airway to see if you can hook out the obstruction using your finger.

- If this is not successful, turn the patient onto his/her side.
- Give four to five blows between the shoulder blades.
- If this fails, kneel astride the casualty and give abdominal thrusts, using the heel of one hand just below the rib cage and pressing sharply inwards and upwards five times.
- If this still fails, **dial 999** and begin resuscitation while waiting for the ambulance (➡ CPR page 306).

5. If YOU are choking

If you can cough, you can take in air, in which case you are not actually choking – coughing will clear any small crumbs, etc. that may have gone down your airway. If you cannot cough, however, you *are* choking. If no one is available to help, you can do the Heimlich manoeuvre on yourself. There are two methods:

1) Place one fist (the weaker one) against your upper abdomen, just below the rib-cage. Your thumb should be pressing against you. Cover the fist with your stronger hand and thrust upwards several times until the object is dislodged.

2) Lean forwards onto something like the back of a chair, positioning it just below your ribcage and thrust your whole body down onto it until the obstruction is cleared.

You should then seek medical attention straight away, even if you feel well. **Phone NHS Direct** for advice. If you feel unwell, **dial 999** to be on the safe side.

For more details, and for other situations when you can use the Heimlich manoeuvre, see www.heimlichinstitute.org.

If you are on your own with any choking patient, call for help while administering the above techniques. Ask someone to dial 999.

Diabetic emergency

Although diabetes is usually a life-long condition that patients control using drugs and diet, sometimes an emergency situation can arise. If someone you know has diabetes and seems to be drowsy or appears to faint, treat this as a diabetic emergency.

999

➤ If the casualty is conscious and able to swallow, immediately give sugar, a sugary drink, chocolate or other sweet food.

➤ If the casualty is unconscious, do not give anything by mouth. Treat for unconsciousness (➡ page 306).

➤ Dial 999 immediately.

Electric shock

999

➤ Never touch the casualty unless you are sure that the electric current is no longer in contact.

➤ If there is a chance that the electric current is still in contact or a danger, if possible switch off the electricity supply.

➤ If this is not possible, remove the casualty from the electrical source using something like a dry wooden or plastic brush handle, or a piece of dry clothing.

➤ If the patient's breathing and heartbeat have stopped, begin resuscitation immediately (➡ CPR page 306).

➤ If the patient is breathing but unconscious put them in the recovery position (➡ page 309).

➤ Treat any burns (➡ page 290) and treat for shock (➡ page 305).

➤ In all cases the casualty must be taken to hospital – dial 999.

Epileptic fit

There is very little you need to do while someone is having an epileptic fit. It is not really an emergency at all, but I have included it because it can be very frightening for someone witnessing it. The main aim is to keep the patient safe. Do not leave the patient alone until he has recovered fully.

➤ If the patient starts to fall down, try to support him while falling, and help him lie down safely.

➤ Clear a space around the person and loosen clothing around the neck. Place something soft under the head.

➤ When convulsions have stopped, place the patient in the recovery position (➡ page 309).

➤ DO NOT move the patient unless there is danger.

➤ DO NOT forcibly restrain the patient unless there is danger.

➤ DO NOT try to wake the patient and do not put anything in his/her mouth.

An epileptic fit can be quite mild – it may look as if the person is simply daydreaming. In a minor attack, stay with him/her until you are certain that recovery is complete.

Fractures/dislocation

Sometimes it's obvious that a bone or joint is broken or dislocated. Sometimes it isn't. If fracture or dislocation is possible, assume that this is what has happened and treat accordingly.

999

➤ Call an ambulance – unless the patient can walk and you are able to drive the patient to A&E. (This might be the case for a limb such as a wrist.)

➤ Try to prevent all unnecessary movement of the limb. Do not try to move the patient or the affected limb while waiting for an ambulance, except to let the patient rest comfortably.

➤ If the person has any other problems, such as difficulty breathing (➡ page 288), severe bleeding (➡ page 289) or unconsciousness (➡ page 306), treat these first.

➤ Gently support the injured part by hand, or using any nearby item such as a book or thick pad of clothing, while waiting for the ambulance.

➤ In the case of an arm or leg, if possible or if you have to wait a long time for help, try to immobilize the injured part by securing it to another part of the body with padding and bandages. Your aim is to prevent all unnecessary movement of the joint. If the joint is already supported, for example because it is resting on the floor, leave well alone.

➤ Do not attempt to put a dislocated joint back – you can make it worse.

➤ Treat for shock (➡ page 305).

➤ A broken bone is an emergency, even if the patient seems to be coping well – in some cases, the break could be pressing on the blood supply and this could cause more damage if not treated immediately.

Head injury

Any head injury can be serious, even if the patient is conscious. Seek medical treatment immediately.

999

Dos and Don'ts

➤ Do treat unconsciousness (➡ page 306).

➤ Do treat shock (➡ page 305).

➤ Do treat any other injuries, such as bleeding (➡ page 289) or fracture (➡ page 297).

➤ Do keep the patient warm and comfortable until help arrives.

➤ Do not try to move the patient if there is a possibility of neck or spinal injury.

➤ Do not give the patient anything to eat, drink or smoke.

➤ If the injury is small and the patient did not lose consciousness even for a second, watch for signs of:

• drowsiness;

• nausea or vomiting;

• confusion;

• unusual anger or violent behaviour;

• anything unusual.

In any of these cases, seek medical attention.

Heart attack

You can save someone's life by knowing what to do during a heart attack. Many suspected heart attacks turn out to be nothing more than indigestion or a strained chest muscle, so try not to panic and do reassure the patient that there is plenty of time to get to hospital. Tell the patient that help is on the way and that you know how to look after him/her – which you do, because it's set out for you here:

999

➤ Dial 999 and explain that you think someone is having a heart attack.

➤ While waiting for the ambulance, reassure the patient.

➤ Gently support the patient with pillows, placing him/her in a half-sitting position with knees bent.

➤ Prevent the patient from making unnecessary movements.

➤ Loosen any tight clothing around the neck, chest and waist.

➤ Treat for shock (➡ page 305).

➤ If the casualty is unconscious and heartbeat and breathing have stopped, begin CPR immediately and continue till the ambulance arrives or breathing starts (➡ page 306).

➤ If the casualty is unconscious but breathing normally, place in the recovery position (➡ page 309) and check pulse rate regularly.

Meningitis

Meningitis is a serious illness. It can lead to death or permanent disability. In most cases, however, it does not. The outcome mainly depends on two things:

➤ whether it is viral (more common and less serious) or bacterial (less common but more dangerous);

➤ how quickly hospital treatment begins.

You need to know the symptoms. The problem is that meningitis often seems like flu at first and can progress quickly. If you or someone you know has flu symptoms, be aware of any changes that might occur and get urgent medical help if you are worried. Call NHS Direct if in doubt (➡ page 231). But remember – most people with flu symptoms turn out to have flu.

These are the symptoms which should alert you to the *possibility* of meningitis. The starred symptoms are especially important. Do not wait for *all* of the symptoms – any combination of them *could* be enough. But remember – it may well *not* be meningitis. It is simply better to be safe than sorry.

In adults and older children

High temperature, with any of the following:

➤ severe headache*;

➤ neck stiffness (unable to touch chin to chest)*;

➤ vomiting* and/or diarrhoea;

➤ aversion to bright light*;

➤ drowsiness*;

➤ fits*;

➤ confusion*;

> a rash that does not fade when a glass is pressed to it*
  (➡ **Tumbler test** below).
> joint or muscle pains;
> stomach cramps.

In babies and infants under two years old

Any combination of the following:
> high temperature/fever*(possibly with cold hands and feet);
> vomiting and refusing feeds;
> high-pitched moaning*;
> whimpering cry;
> blank, staring expression*;
> pale, blotchy complexion*;
> floppiness*;
> dislike of being handled*;
> neck retraction with arching of back*;
> convulsions*;
> difficult to wake*;
> lethargic*;
> tense or bulging fontanelle* (soft spot on head);
> a rash that does not fade when a glass is pressed to it*
  (➡ **Tumbler test** below).

Tumbler test

Sometimes, the bacteria that cause bacterial meningitis may cause septicaemia (blood poisoning). A rash of purple-red spots may appear, starting as a cluster of tiny blood spots, which join together to look like fresh bruises.

Press the side of a clear drinking glass onto the rash or bruises and check if they fade. If they do *not* fade, you should suspect septicaemia. This is a medical emergency and you should get the patient to hospital immediately – dial 999 if this is the quickest way. In a small number of cases the rash may fade at first but may later change into one that does not fade. Repeat the test every hour if it is negative at first.

Nosebleed

Nosebleeds are common and most stop quite quickly. Here's what to do to help a nosebleed stop:

➤ Make the patient sit down with head leaning forward.
➤ Pinch the nose just below the bridge (main bony part just below eye-level) for about 10 minutes. Ask the patient to breathe through his/her mouth and not to speak, swallow (if possible) or cough.
➤ If available, hold ice packs over the nose area.
➤ If the bleeding does not stop, pinch the bridge of the nose for another 10 minutes.

999 **If the bleeding still does not stop**
➤ Seek immediate medical help.
➤ While waiting for help, continue alternating nose-pinching with ice packs.
➤ Keep the patient calm and still.

Poisoning

There are many forms of poisoning, including alcohol or drug overdoses and carbon monoxide poisoning. You must get emergency medical help as soon as possible. Different types of poisoning need different treatment and you could make things worse by doing the wrong thing.

999 If you suspect that someone may have taken an overdose of pills, do not wait to be sure before getting help. Paracetamol can be harmful in even quite small overdoses and the patient may seem quite well and alert. Hospital treatment is essential, quickly.

Things you can safely do while waiting for help:
➤ If breathing and heartbeat have stopped, begin CPR (➡ page 306).
➤ Be careful not to contaminate yourself with anything on the casualty's mouth. (If there is a risk of this, close the mouth and breathe into the nose instead.)
➤ If the patient is unconscious but breathing, put in the recovery position (➡ page 309).
➤ If the patient is conscious, try to find out exactly what has happened – he/she may fall unconscious later.
➤ If the patient is conscious, you may give sips of milk or water to drink if the lips or mouth are burning.
➤ Do not force the patient to vomit as this may cause further harm.
➤ In the case of inhaling a poisonous gas, get the patient into the fresh air.

➤ In the case of absorbing poison through the skin, try to wash away any residual chemical that may be on the skin. Take care: wear rubber gloves.

➤ Give or tell the medical staff anything that may help identify the poison. For example, if you found pills or an empty bottle, take these to the hospital with the patient. Tell the absolute truth – forget about protecting a secret: this is someone's life and the medical staff can only do the right thing if they have all the information.

Shock

Shock happens after most accidents, including burns. The body responds to an accident or injury by quickly diverting blood to the heart, away from the limbs and head.

Signs

➤ Pale, sweaty face.

➤ Cold, clammy skin.

➤ Breathing may be shallow and rapid.

➤ Patient may feel weak, faint, anxious, restless, nauseous and could vomit.

➤ In severe cases, the patient can become unconscious.

Treatment

➤ If breathing and heartbeat have stopped, begin resuscitation (CPR) immediately (➡ page 306).

➤ If the casualty is conscious, but breathing is difficult and they seem likely to vomit or become unconscious, place them in the recovery position (➡ page 309). Then continue to check breathing and pulse every 10 minutes.

➤ If possible find out the cause of shock and treat it.

➤ If the casualty is conscious and is not suffering any of the above:

• Lie the casualty down.

• Raise and support the legs.

• Keep the casualty warm and loosen tight clothing.

• Call for medical assistance – **dial 999** if severe (for example, vomiting or losing consciousness) or **call NHS Direct** (➡ page 231) if less severe.

• DO NOT give the casualty a hot water bottle, or allow him/her to eat, drink or smoke.

Unconsciousness and CPR

Unconsciousness, for whatever reason, should always be treated as an emergency.

999
> Shout firmly, asking 'Are you all right?' If there is no response, then:
> Shout for help. If someone comes, get them to dial 999 while you continue with the following steps. If no one comes, dial 999 and then act by yourself.
> Follow the ABC steps below.

ABC is the easy way to remember the order of actions in CPR CPR is the system for re-starting and maintaining breathing and heartbeat.

NOTE: ➤ **Adult:** Call for help before starting CPR.
➤ **Child:** Carry out CPR for 1 minute before calling for help.

A – Airway   B – Breathing   C – Circulation (heart pumping blood)

A. Airway (mouth, throat and windpipe)
- Open the mouth and check for obstruction.
- Use a finger to sweep the airway clear – but be very careful not to push anything further down the throat.
- Tilt the chin upwards.

B.   Breathing
- Check to see if the chest is moving and feel for breath.
- If the patient is not breathing after 10 seconds, breathe two times into his/her mouth, holding the nose shut.
- Then check circulation.

C.   Circulation
- Check for pulse by pressing under the jawbone to the side of windpipe.
- If you aren't sure, and if there is no movement or coughing (it can be difficult to tell when you are under stress) assume the heart has stopped and continue with steps towards CPR (see below).

CPR

For an adult
- ➤ Place the heel of one hand over the patient's lower breast bone. Place your other hand on top, pointing the same way, and lock your fingers together.
- ➤ With arms straight, press down firmly fifteen times. The speed should be at the rate of two compressions per second.
- ➤ Return to the patient's head and give two more breaths.
- ➤ Then give a further fifteen compressions.
- ➤ Repeat the cycle of two breaths followed by fifteen compressions until help arrives.
- ➤ Do not give up.

If the person starts to breathe unaided, place them in the recovery position.

For a child
There are two important differences in giving CPR to a child:

➤ When doing chest compressions, use only one hand and do not press too hard.

➤ Give one breath after every five compressions (instead of the 2:15 for an adult).

For a baby less than one year old

There are three important differences:

➤ When giving breaths, place your mouth over the baby's nose *and* mouth together.

➤ Use only two fingers for the chest compressions, and at a slightly faster rate than two per second.

➤ Give one breath after every five compressions.

Continue with CPR until either help arrives or breathing and heart rate/pulse returns.

Once the breathing and heart rate/pulse returns, place the patient in the recovery position (➡ page 309).

Recovery position

This is the safest position for someone who is unconscious but breathing. It allows easier breathing and means that if the patient vomits there is no danger of choking.

> **NOTE:** If you suspect a spinal or neck injury, do not move the patient into the recovery position.

To put a person in the recovery position
- ➤ Place the patient on his/her back and kneel on one side.
- ➤ Lift the chin slightly so that the airway is open.
- ➤ Position the patient's arm on your side so as to make a right angle with his body, with elbow bent and palm facing out.
- ➤ Position the patient's opposite arm across the chest, with back of his hand against the cheek nearer to you.
- ➤ Pull up the patient's knee joint (the leg further from you) so that it is bent with the foot flat on the ground (➡ Figure 1 overleaf).
- ➤ Roll the patient over in this position towards your side.
- ➤ By tilting the patient's head back ensure that the airway is still open (➡ Figure 2 overleaf).
- ➤ Adjust the uppermost leg so that the hip and knee are at right angles and the patient is in a stable position (➡ Figure 3 overleaf).

This is complicated if you are reading it *during* an emergency. Practise it when there is no emergency, then you won't have to think.

Figure 1

Figure 2

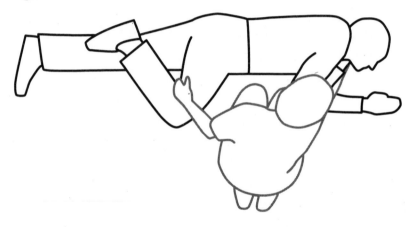

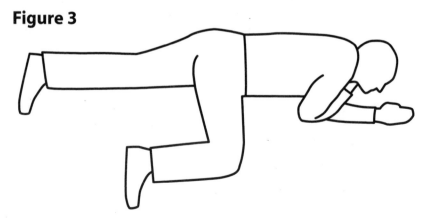

Other emergencies

Burglary/crime

999
- ➤ If you suspect someone is in your house while you are there, or if you come back to your house and find evidence of forced entry, or anything that makes you suspicious, take no chances: dial 999. Don't enter the house on your own.
- ➤ If you discover that you have been the victim of crime, do not touch or move anything. Dial 999.

NOTE: If something is stolen from you, always report it to the police, even if you feel they can do nothing about it. There are two reasons:

- ➤ The police need to know about patterns of crime, so that they can target resources to a particular area.
- ➤ If you claim on your insurance, you will need to have reported the incident to the police. If it is not an emergency, you do not need to do this immediately. Just do it as soon as you can.
- ➤ In the above circumstance, do not dial 999, but phone your nearest police station.

Car accident

➤ If you are involved in an accident or are present when one happens, stop as soon as you safely can.

➤ The hard shoulder on a motorway is a very dangerous place – if you have to stop here, get out of your car if possible and stand away from the road.

999 **Dial 999 if**
➤ Anyone is injured, even slightly.
➤ One of the cars is blocking the traffic or in a dangerous place.
➤ Any of the cars cannot be driven. If in doubt, do not drive a damaged car.

➤ Do not attempt to get a seriously injured person out of a car, unless there is a danger of fire.

➤ If you are able to, move to safety and warn oncoming traffic. If you have a hazard triangle, place it twenty metres behind the accident.

Insurance/legal aspects of a car crash

Obey these rules to keep within the law:

➤ Always stop after an accident.
➤ Check for damage to vehicles and injuries to people or animals.
➤ Do not get involved in a conversation with the other driver about whose fault it was. This is for your insurance companies to sort out.
➤ Exchange details (name, address, phone number, vehicle

registration number and insurance details) with all others involved. If you do not stop, or cannot provide any details (➡ point 7 below), you must report the accident to the police within 24 hours. If a person or animal has been injured, or property damaged (other than your own), then you *must* report it if you could not give all the details at the time of the accident.

➤ Make a note of the other people involved and the vehicles (colour, make, model and registration). If possible, make a note of the position of the vehicles before any are moved.

➤ If there were any witnesses, take their contact details too.

➤ If you are faced with aggression from another driver and are afraid to give your name and address, call the police and give your details to them. You are obliged to give your name and address but, if you feel threatened, the police will be sympathetic.

➤ If the police are called and you think that you may have been at fault, ask if you can arrange to give a statement at a later date. You can then prepare and also instruct a solicitor if necessary.

NOTE: In any instance where the police are called, they will breathalize both/all drivers. Don't be offended by this – it is routine.

➤ As soon as you can after the accident, sit quietly and write out your recollection of exactly what happened.

➤ Report the accident to your insurers. (If the damage is only to your car, and is only minor, you might decide not to claim on your insurance ➡ page 48).

➤ Anyone who was injured in the accident, even if only slightly, should see a doctor as soon as possible.

The insurance companies will decide who was to blame and therefore which company will pay out. If it was your fault, your insurance company will pay for the damage to both vehicles. You will be asked to provide a detailed description of what happened, and you will probably have to draw a diagram. You do not have to decide whose fault it was. Simply explain clearly what happened and why. If it was your fault, the insurance company will still pay as long as you have a valid policy and have obeyed its conditions. The insurance companies want to know whose fault it is because they need to decide which of them pays.

Fire

Very minor fires

Never take risks with fire. Only attempt to extinguish the most minor ones yourself.

➤ Smother a chip pan or saucepan fire with a thick blanket (have a fire blanket in the kitchen at all times and make sure everyone knows where it is – they are cheap, and available from DIY stores and some large supermarkets).

➤ Never put water on a fire that has fat in it – such as frying-pan or chip pan.

➤ Do not assume that a fire has gone out – they can retain heat and relight if you are not very careful. Call the fire brigade if you are not absolutely sure that the fire is out or if you think any electricity, gas or water pipes may have been damaged.

If someone's clothes are on fire

999

➤ Make the person lie down immediately – flames travel upwards, so lying down gives them less chance to burn.

➤ Roll the person over to extinguish flames. Roll him/her in a blanket or rug if handy. If not, use a cushion, coat or any thick cloth to extinguish the flames.

➤ Dial 999. Meanwhile, check for burns (➡ page 290 for emergency burns section).

For other fires

999 For any fire other than the smallest ones, and any of the above fires that you cannot immediately put out:

➤ Shout to alert all other members of the house. Get any children out of their rooms.

➤ Leave the house, closing all windows and doors behind you, but do not go into the burning area.

➤ Dial 999 – if possible from a mobile phone. If you can't phone, alert the nearest neighbour.

➤ Never go back into the house to retrieve anything. Never go upstairs if you are already downstairs.

➤ If you have to go through smoke, get a towel/face cloth, soak it in water and place over your mouth and nose as you leave the house. Smoke kills more people than flames do.

➤ If you are trapped, stay in one room with the door shut; wedge towels (wet if possible) under the door. Shout and wave out of an open window to get help.

➤ Smoke rises so the clearest air will be at floor level – if there is smoke in the room, stay with your face close to the floor.

➤ Never use lifts when there is fire or smoke in the building.

Gas

If you smell gas

➤ **Never** light a flame – don't smoke or light a match.

➤ **Never** switch any electrical switches on or off – they can make a spark which might be enough to ignite gas in the air.

➤ Put out naked flames throughout the house – gas fires, candles, gas hobs, etc.

➤ Open doors and windows.

➤ If you still smell gas, get everyone away from the building.

➤ Turn off the gas at the mains (➡ page 130).

➤ Phone 0800 111 999 – Transco's emergency number.

Homelessness

If you find yourself homeless, this is an emergency. Sleeping on the streets or in any public place is *never* the answer – it is dangerous for you and will not provide the help you need to solve the problem in the long term. Here are your better options – choose whichever will work for you:

➤ Phone a friend. Yes, I know, it's hard to do this sometimes. After all, you don't want to impose on them. But if a friend of yours was suddenly homeless and didn't phone you, wouldn't you be embarrassed? Promise to find a better solution – and then do so.

➤ Phone the council housing department. The council is obliged to find you emergency accommodation if you need it. It won't be instant luxury (well, OK, actually it probably won't be luxury at all), but it will be a bed and a roof. Better than nothing, and it will do until you find somewhere.

➤ Contact Shelter – phone their UK-wide helpline, which is open 24 hours a day on 0808 800 4444. They may have a Housing Advice Centre in your region. Even if they don't, they will give you instant emergency advice and help.

Loss of wallet/ handbag/credit cards

If you think you may have lost a credit card, you need to 'stop' the card or cards as soon as possible.

- ➤ Phone the number which the credit card company will have given you.
- ➤ If you can't find it, phone their telephone helpline.
- ➤ If they do not have one or you do not know it or the line is closed, do not panic – as long as you can phone within 24 hours, you will not be blamed.
- ➤ Report the loss to the police and ask what you should do. (This is not a 999 situation – your nearest police station is the place to phone or visit.)

If you have lost cash, unfortunately you may well not get it back. Also unfortunately, it usually won't be covered by insurance.

- ➤ You should still report it to the nearest local police station.
- ➤ Report it to all the shops in the area where you might have lost it.
- ➤ If you lost it on public transport, tell the transport company.

For any other loss

- ➤ Report it to your nearest police station.
- ➤ If your mobile phone was stolen, inform your phone company *straight away* – otherwise you will be liable for any calls made on the phone (unless you have insurance for this).
- ➤ If there were items of value, consider claiming against

your insurance if you have it (➡ page 45). Usually you will not receive the first £50 or £100, depending on your policy, so it's usually only worth claiming for a loss greater than that.

➤ If your house keys were in the bag with anything identifying where you live (or name and place of work – someone could use that to get your home address), you should have the locks on your house changed. And tell the police. Call a locksmith – you'll find them in the Yellow Pages. You should be able to claim for the cost of this on your insurance.

➤ Inform your students' union if you are a student.

➤ Inform your Neighbourhood Watch if there is one.

➤ If the theft occurred at or near your home, tell other residents and neighbours.

Water leak

➤ Turn the mains tap/stop valve off first (➡ page 125), to stop more water going into the storage tank. (All taps turn off clockwise.)

➤ Turn off any other stop valves, usually found under the kitchen sink.

➤ If the leak does not stop in a few seconds, open all other cold taps everywhere in the house/flat – this is to drain the cold water storage tank.

➤ Do *not* turn on the hot taps.

➤ Switch off central heating and hot water system and turn off any electric fires.

➤ Now call a plumber.

Water coming through a ceiling/roof

➤ Place bowls or buckets underneath to catch drips.

➤ If the water is coming through a light fitting, do not touch it or try to use the light until the water has gone.

➤ It is possible that plaster may come down. However, this does not usually happen. Remove objects from underneath the ceiling, just in case. Once the source of water has been stopped and water has finished dripping, allow the ceiling to dry slowly (do not try to speed the process using hairdryers, though putting the heating on a medium setting would be fine). If the plaster seems to sag, you would be better calling a plasterer – the mess of an expert taking plaster down is nothing compared with the mess it will make if it falls of its own accord.

Index

A

A&E (Accident and Emergency Department) 206, 297
ABC (airway, breathing and circulation) 283, 306–7
abdominal thrusts 292, 293
accidental damage 47
accidents
   and alcohol 250
   car accidents 269–70, 313–15
   first aid 221–3
   where to get help 205–6
   see also emergencies
accommodation 61–87, 93
   buying a property 64
   different types of 64–7
   homelessness 80, 319
   household bills 81–4
   student accommodation 78
   Troubleshoot 87
   see also rented accommodation;
     shared accommodation
acupressure 218
affinity cards 31
AIDS/HIV 256
air fresheners 140
air miles 30–1
airers (clothes) 99
airlocks in radiators 128
alcohol 250–2
   avoiding or minimizing risks of 250–1
   drinking and driving 252, 266, 269
   and first aid 222
   health risks of 250
   and the law 266
   and medicines 203–4
   minimizing the effects of 252
   poisoning 303
   and sex 250, 254
   spiked drinks 252, 254–6
   and stress 229
   and travelling abroad 260
   working out units of 251–2
allergies 207, 210
   food allergies/intolerance 218
anti-bacterial spray 102
antibiotics 193, 203, 204, 214, 215
ants 131
APAs (Adopted Practical Adults) 108, 117, 127, 130

appearance, and job interviews 236–7
APR (annual percentage rate) 18, 25–6, 30, 32
arms, fractured 297
aromatherapy (essential) oils 201, 213–14, 216
arrests, being arrested 277–8
aspirin 201–2, 210, 217
Assured Tenancies 73, 74
asthma 101, 188, 202, 210
   attacks 288
   prescriptions for 194, 195

B

babies
   choking 291–2
   giving CPR to 308
   meningitis 301
bank accounts 16–23
   bank charges 18, 21
   bank statements 22
   choosing a bank 16–18
   ethical banking 20
   interest 24, 25–6
   interest-paying current accounts 18
   Internet banking 19
   loans 18
   overdraft facilities 17, 37
   overdrawn 17, 21
   references 72
   telephone banking services 18
   writing a cheque 22–3
bath edges
   filling cracks beside 121
   removing mildew from 120
bathrooms 69
   cleaning 107
   and safety 137, 138
beer, units of 251
bees 131
benefits (state) 58
   claiming 238, 240
   Housing Benefit 58, 82, 83, 240
   and prescriptions 194
bicarbonate of soda 105, 119, 140, 154, 155, 156
bicycle insurance 47
bill payments 38
   by direct debit or standing order 36–7
   household bills 81–4

INDEX

council tax 82–3
  problems with paying 83–4
  standing charges 82
  television licence 82
  utility 81–2, 84
  leaving accommodation 79
  responsibility for 74
  in shared accommodation 85
biological washing power/liquid 97–8
bleach 102–3, 104–5, 120
bleeding wounds
  emergencies 289
  first aid for 222
blocked toilets 128
blown fuses 111–14
boilers
  and carbon monoxide poisoning 137
  servicing 132
breathing
  and CPR 306–7
  and relaxation 228–9
breathing difficulties 288
  and fractures 297
  and poisoning 303
  and shock 305
budgeting 51–5
  for accommodation 67
  cheap eating 174–5
  debt problems 54–5
  outgoings (expenses) 51–2
    cutting 52–4
  student discounts 52
building society accounts 24
buildings insurance 45, 74
  rented accommodation 74
burglar alarms 46, 48
burglaries 253, 257, 259
  emergencies 312
burns
  and electric shock 295
  first aid for 223
  severe 290
burst pipes 125, 126–7
Business Link 241
buying a property 64

C

CAB (Citizen's Advice Bureau) 59, 87
  and benefits 58
  and consumer law 271, 272, 274
  and credit rating 41

and debt problems 55
and the law 265, 278
and rented accommodation 64, 65,
  73
candles, preventing fires 136
cannabis 267–8
carbon monoxide poisoning 136–7,
  138, 303
carpets
  chemicals in 101
  stain removal 104–5
cars
  accidents 269–70, 313–15
  drinking and driving 252, 266, 269
  insurance 45–6, 48, 269, 314–15
  and the law 269–70, 313–15
  theft from 257
cash machines, withdrawals from 17,
  32, 258
CCJs (County Court Judgements), and
  credit rating 39, 41
ceilings
  painting 121
  water coming through 322
central heating 69
chemical-free living 139–40
chemicals
  and cleaning products 94
  and house dust 101
cheques
  stopping 134
  writing a cheque 22–3
chewing-gum, removing 106
children
  choking 292
  giving CPR to a child 307–8
  meningitis 300–1
chip pan fires 316
chlamydia 200
choking 291–3
  babies 291–2
  young children 292
circuit-breakers/power-breakers 118
Citizen's Advice Bureau see CAB
  (Citizen's Advice Bureau)
cleaning 94–107
  and chemical-free living 139–40
  clothes 96–100
  detergents/disinfectants/bleach 102–3
  dusting 101
  and the environment 94–5
  freezers 157

fridges 155
hobs and ovens 154
how often to clean 107
on leaving accommodation 79
in shared accommodation 85
sheets 103–4
stain removal 102–3, 104–6
vacuum cleaners 103
clothes cleaning 96–100
dry-cleaning 100
drying clothes 98–9
laundrettes 99–100
laundry symbols and instructions 96–7
washing powder/liquid 97–8
clothes on fire 316
cloths, kitchen 104, 164
colds and flu *see* flu
confidence, and job applications 236, 240
consciousness, loss of 207, 208, 222
Consumer Credit Counselling Service 59
consumer law 271–5
caveat emptor 274
cooling-off periods 273
delivered goods 275
disagreements with a shop/company 274
doorstep traders 273
reading the small print 274–5
refunds/replacements 271, 272, 274
returning goods 271–2
contents/possessions insurance 45, 46–8
accidental damage 47
conditions of 46–7, 48
'new-for-old' cover 47
contraception 194, 198–9, 200
emergency 194, 198–9
cooking 176–8
beating/whisking 176
browning 176–7
cookbooks 176
cooking methods 177
and food safety 166–8
fruit and vegetables in 173
liquids 177
salt in 177
sauces 178
in shared accommodation 85
simmering 154, 177
stir-fries 173, 178

cooling food 167–8
coughs 214–15
council tax 67, 82–3
councils *see* local councils
CPR (Cardio Pulmonary Resuscitation) 283
and choking 293
and heart attacks 299
and poisoning 303
and shock 305
cracks, filling 121
credit cards 29–35
0% credit cards 32–3, 55
advantages of 30–1
affinity cards 31
annual fees 21, 31
card protection and fraud 33–5
and consumer law 272
credit cashback cards 31
and credit rating 32, 33, 41
and debt problems 55
minimum payments on 31–2, 41
missing 33–4, 258, 320
store cards 29, 30
credit rating 32, 33, 39–41
checking or changing 39–41
factors affecting 39
guidelines for improving 40–1
letters of disassociation 40
crime prevention 257–8
Crime Prevention Officers 258, 259
customers *see* consumer law
CVs 236, 237, 238–9

D

date rape 254–6
debit cards 28, 30
debt problems 54–5
defrosting freezers 156–7
delivered goods, and consumer law 275
Delta cards 18, 22, 34
dentists 224–5
depression 227, 229
descaling shower heads/kettles 120
detergents 102, 104
diabetes 194
diabetic emergency 294
diarrhoea 215–17
direct debits 32, 36–7, 77
rent payments 77
Disabled Person's Tax Credit 194

disinfectant 102
dislocation/fracture 289, 297
DIY *see* household repairs (DIY)
doctors *see* GPs (general practitioners)
door locks 77
drills
    drill 'bits' 118
    electric 115, 116, 117–18
drugs
    drug rape 254–6
    illegal 254–6
        classes of 267–8
    overdoses 303
    spiked drinks 252, 254–6
    see also medicines
dry-cleaning 100
drying clothes 98–9
dust and dusting 101

E

E111 48, 261
echinacea 201, 214
eczema 195
eggs
    storing 166
    testing for freshness 167
electric drills 115, 116
    using 117–18
electric shock 295
electricians 112, 113, 133
electricity 109, 112, 113, 114
    bills 81
        cutting 52, 53–4
    circuit-breakers/power-breakers 118
    cutting bills 52, 53–4
    extension cables 118
    faulty electrical equipment 113, 136
    finding cables in walls 117
    fuses 109
        blown 111–14
        fuse wire 109, 112
        mains fuse box 112, 124
        trip switches 112, 113, 124
    heavy and light power users 114
    in the kitchen 151–61
    lighting circuit 124
    meters 76, 125
    power cuts 159
    repairing household items 114
    replacing a light bulb 109–11
    and safety 137–8

safety certificates 70–1
sockets 124
    overloaded 113, 114
    switching off at the mains 112, 124
e-mail scams 57
emergencies 9, 281–322
    burglary/crime 312
    car accidents 313–15
    faked 999 calls 259
    fire 316–17
    gas 318
    homelessness 319
    loss of wallet/handbag/credit cards
        320–1
    medical 206–7, 208, 287–310
        asthma attack/breathing difficulties
        288
        bleeding 289
        burns 290
        choking 291–3
        diabetic 294
        electric shock 295
        epileptic fit 296
        and first aid 221–3
        fractures/dislocation 297
        head injuries 298
        heart attack 299
        meningitis 300–1
        nosebleed 302
        poisoning 303–4
        and the recovery position 309–10
        shock 305
        unconsciousness and CPR 306–8
    water leak 322
emergency contraception 194, 198–9
emulsion paints 121, 122
the environment, and cleaning 94–5
epilepsy 194
    emergencies 296
essential oils 201, 213–14, 216
estate agencies, renting through 66
ethical banking 20
eucalyptus oil 213, 214
European Union countries
    and travel insurance 48–9
    travelling in 261
evening classes 228
evening primrose oil 189
eviction 74–5
exercise 186–7
    and stress 229
extended warranties 49–50

extension cables 118
eyes 226

F

Family Planning Association 199
fan ovens 152
farmers' markets 173
fever 209–10, 212, 214, 217
fire 316–17
  clothes on fire 316
  escaping from 70, 316–17
  preventing fires 136
first aid 221–3
fish, raw 155, 158, 163, 168
fish oils 189
Fixed Term Assured Shorthold Tenancy
  Agreements 73
flexible filler 121
flies, and food 165
flu 211–15
  self-treatment 212–14
  symptoms 211–12
  vaccinations 188
  when to seek help 214–15
food 143–79
  and cheap eating 174–5
  chemical-free 139, 140
  eating
    balanced diet 169–70
    eating out 188
    fruit and vegetables 172–3
    and sickness/diarrhoea 216
  essentials
    freezer 147
    fridge 147
    kitchen equipment 148–9
    quick meals 147
    store cupboard 146, 147
  fast food/ready meals 169, 170
  frozen 157, 158–9, 174
  hygiene and safety 162–8, 187
    cooking 166–8
    cooling 167–8
    frozen food 158–9
    handling food 163
    leftovers 165
    personal hygiene 162–3, 216
    reheating 167
    shopping hygiene 168
    storing food 164–6
  microwaving 160–1

sell-by/use by/best before dates 164
  and shared accommodation 83
  special diets 172
  Troubleshoot 179
  vegans 172
  vegetarians 170–1
  see also kitchens
food allergies/intolerance 218
food poisoning 162, 167, 188
  hygiene 216
  self-treatment 215–16
  when to seek help 217
Foyer Federation 80
fractures/dislocation 289, 297
fraud, credit card 33–5
freezers 156–9
  defrosting 156–7
  foods not to freeze 158–9
  freezing food 157, 158–9, 165
  and power cuts 159
  temperature 157
  thawing food 157, 158
fridge-freezers 156
fridges 155–6
  and food safety 155, 164, 165
  foods to keep in 166
  temperature 155, 165
friendships 228, 230
frozen pipes, preventing 129–30
fruit 172–3, 186
  storing 166
furnished accommodation 66–7, 69
  inventories 76
  reporting damage 79
fuses 109
  blown 111–14
  fuse wire 109, 112
  mains fuse box 112, 124
  trip switches 112, 113, 124

G

gambling, and debt problems 55
gas 130, 138
  bills 81
    cutting 52, 54
  carbon monoxide poisoning 136–7,
    138, 303
  emergencies 318
  hobs 152, 153–4
  mains valve 130
  meter 130

INDEX

ovens 152–3
safety certificates 70–1
GHB 254, 255
ginger, as a remedy for nausea 216
gloss paint 122
glue 109
gluten-free diets 172
going away
  and home security 135
  preventing frozen pipes 130
GPs (general practitioners)
  appointments with 196
  and confidentiality 220
  and immunization/vaccination 188,
    197
  practice nurses 196, 197
  and prescriptions 194
  registering with a GP 190–3
  rights regarding your GP 196–7
  and sexual health 200, 256
  when to consult 205, 219–20
    colds and flu 214–15
    headaches 218
    sickness and diarrhoea 217
    stress and depression 227, 229
grills 151, 152
gross interest 26, 27
grouting, discoloured 120
guests, in shared accommodation 85

H

handbag, loss of 320–1
happiness 187
  factors affecting 227–30
head injuries
  emergencies 298
  first aid for 222
headaches 212, 217–18, 229
  self-treatment 217–18
  symptoms 217
health 181–231
  contraception 194, 198–9, 200
  dental treatment 224–5
  and diet 169–73
  eyes 226
  first aid 221–3
  health risks of alcohol 250
  immune system 186–9, 211, 228
  medicines 201–4
    prescriptions 193–5
  sexual 200

stress 187, 227–30
  Troubleshoot 231
  see also GPs (general practitioners);
    illnesses
heart attacks 299
Heimlich manoeuvre (abdominal
  thrusts) 292, 293
HIV 256
hobs 151, 152, 153–4
holes, filling 121
home security 135, 257
  locking up 77, 85, 135
  loss of house keys 321
  when going away 135
homelessness 80, 319
homosexual rape 259
hospital treatment
  A&E (Accident and Emergency
    Department) 206, 297
  and meningitis 300
household repairs (DIY) 108–41
  and APAs (Adopted Practical Adults)
    108, 117, 127, 130
  calling in the experts 132–4
  descaling 120
  essential tools 109
  filling cracks or holes 121
  nails and screws 109, 115–17
  painting 121–3
  pest control 131
  removing mildew 120
  and safety in the home 135–8
  Troubleshoot 141
  unblocking a sink 119
  see also electricity; gas; tradespeople;
    water
Houses in Multiple Occupation
  (HMOs) 64–5, 82
Housing Associations (HAs) 65
Housing Benefit 58, 82, 83, 240

I

ibuprofen 201–2, 217
illnesses 205–20
  colds and flu 211–15
  fever 209–10, 212, 214, 217
  headaches/migraine 212, 217–18
  post-viral fatigue 212
  sickness/diarrhoea/food poisoning
    215–17
  symptoms 205, 211–12

emergencies 206–7
  when to see a GP 205, 219–20
taking your temperature 209
toxic shock syndrome 208
where to get help 205–6
see also emergencies; GPs (general
  practitioners)
immune system 186–9, 211, 228
immunization 188, 197
Income Support 83, 194, 240
income tax *see* taxation
influenza *see* flu
Inland Revenue 42, 43, 44, 59
  Enquiry Centre 42, 43, 44, 59, 246
insulation 129, 130
insurance 45–50
  brokers 46
  buildings 45, 74
  and burglaries 259, 312
  car 45–6, 48, 269
    accidents 313–15
  contents/possessions 45, 46–8
  excess 46
  extended warranties 49–50
  life/critical illness 45
  loss of wallet/handbag/credit cards
    320–1
  premiums 46
  travel 31, 46, 48–9, 261
interest payments
  and debt problems 55
  tax on 24, 26, 27, 43, 44
interest rates
  bank accounts 18, 25–6
  credit cards 29
Internet
  banking 19
  and credit card fraud 35
interviews
  by the police 277
  for jobs 236–7, 239–40
ISA (Individual Savings Account) 27, 43
IUDs (intrauterine devices) 198

J

job interviews 236–7, 239–40
Jobcentre Plus 237, 238, 240
Jobseeker's Allowance 83, 194, 238,
  240

K

kettles, descaling 120
kitchen cloths 104, 164
kitchens 69
  chip pan/saucepan fires 316
  cleaning/cleaners 103, 107
  electrical items 151–61
    freezers 156–9
    fridges 155–6
    hand mixers 149
    instruction manuals 151
    microwaves 159–61
    ovens and hobs 151–4
  essential kitchen equipment 148–9
  light fittings 111
  useful kitchen equipment 150
  see also food

L

landlords 64–5, 69, 70, 71, 93
  council tax 82
  and household repairs/maintenance
    108, 113, 129
  moving in 76–7
  and property insurance 74
  references 72
  tenancy agreements 65, 69, 73–5
laughter 230
laundrettes 99–100
laundry symbols and instructions 96–7
lavender oil 213
the law 263–79
  and alcohol 266
  and cars 269–70, 313–15
  and customers 271–5
  and drugs 254, 267–8
  noisy neighbours 276
  and tenants 73–5
  Troubleshoot 279
leftover food 165
legs, fractured 297
lemon oil 213
letting agencies, renting through 66
licensees, and tenancy rights 69, 73
life/critical illness insurance 45
light bulbs, replacing 109–11
lights
  and home security 135
  lighting circuit 124
limbs, fractured 297

limescale 120
Local Authority Housing
 Office/Department 87
local councils
 and homelessness 80, 319
 and noisy neighbours 276
 rented accommodation 66

M

Maestro cards 18, 22, 34
mail order goods, and consumer law
 275
mains switches 76
Mastercard 29
matt emulsion 121
mattress protectors 104
meat
 cooking 166–7
 raw 155, 158, 163, 168
medicines 201–4
 and alcohol 203–4
 medicine box items 201
 over-the-counter (OTC) remedies
  195, 213, 215, 217
 painkillers 201–2
 prescription drugs 193–5
 prescriptions 193–5
 safe use of 203–4
meningitis 207, 300–1
 symptoms of 300–1
 tumbler test 301
meter readings 76, 125
meters 76
 electricity 76, 125
 water 81, 129
mice 131
microwaves 159–61
migraine 217–18
 self-treatment 217–18
 symptoms 217
 when to seek help 218
mildew, removing 120
milk, and birds 168
mobile phones
 and driving 269
 extended warranties 50
 guarantee period of 272
 and phone bills 81
 stolen 320
 tariffs 52
 unsolicited text messages 57

money 11–59
 banks 16–26
 benefits 58
 budgeting 51–5
 building society accounts 24
 credit cards 29–35
 credit rating 32, 33, 39–41
 cutting expenses 52–3, 84
 debit cards 28
 direct debits 32, 36–7, 77
 insurance 45–50
 savings accounts 27, 43
 scams 56–7
 standing orders 36–7, 77
 and stress 227
 tax and National Insurance 42–4
 Troubleshoot 59
mortgages 64
muggings 253

N

nails 109, 115
 where not to put 117
National Debtline 59
National Insurance (NI) 41, 42, 243
National Savings accounts 26, 27
neck injuries 309
Neighbourhood Watch 321
net interest 26
NHS Direct 205–6, 210, 214, 217, 218,
 222, 223
NHS (National Health Service)
 and contraception 198–9
 dentists 224–5
 prescriptions 193–5
 Primary Care Trusts (PCTs) 191
 see also GPs (general practitioners)
NI (National Insurance) 41, 42, 243
night-time, walking on your own 252–3
'No More Nails' 109
noise
 noisy neighbours 276
 in shared accommodation 85
nosebleeds 302

O

Omega 3 fish oils 189
opticians 226
OTC (over-the-counter) medicines 195,
 213, 215, 217

for headaches 217
ovens 151–3
  combination ovens 159–60
  microwaves 159–61
over-the-counter (OTC) medicines *see*
  OTC (over-the-counter) medicines

P

P60/P45 forms 243
painkillers 201–2
painting 121–3
panic attacks 229
paracetamol 201, 202, 210
  and flu 212–13
  and headaches 217
  safe use of 203
parents, buying a property with 64
passports 261
PAYE (Pay as You Earn) 42, 43
paying bills *see* bill payments
peppermint essential oil 216
personal hygiene, and food 162–3, 216
personal safety 235, 247–62
  and alcohol 250–2
  getting home safely 252–3
  travelling abroad 260–1
  Troubleshoot 262
personality, negative outlook 227
pest control 131
pharmacies 205, 217
pill, 'morning-after' 198–9
pipes, frozen 129–30
plasterboard walls, putting screws in
  115, 116
plumbers 119, 129, 130, 132, 133, 322
plungers, unblocking sinks 119
PMS (pre-menstrual syndrome) 189
poisoning 303–4
  see also food poisoning
police
  being arrested 277–8
  and car accidents 314
  Crime Prevention Officers 258, 259
  and drug rape 256
  loss of wallet/handbag/credit cards
    320–1
  and noisy neighbours 276
  and rape 259
  reporting crime 258–9, 312
post, redirecting 79
post-viral fatigue 212

potatoes 166
pre-menstrual syndrome (PMS) 189
prescriptions 193–5
  OTC drugs on 195
  paying for 194
  pre-paid certificates 195
  prescription-only drugs 193
privacy, in shared accommodation 85
Pyrex dishes 153, 160

R

radiators, airlocks in 128
rape 259
  drug rape 254–6
rats 131
recovery position 309–10
  and electric shock 295
  and poisoning 303
  and shock 305
references, providing for landlords 72
reheating food 167
relaxation
  and breathing 228–9
  and headaches 217–18
rented accommodation
  advertisements for 68
  Assured Tenancies 73, 74
  bill payments 74
  deposits 70, 73, 76–7
    return of 79
  eviction from 74–5
  finding 68–71
    advertisements 68
    questions to ask 69–70
    viewing the property 70–1
  Fixed Term Assured Shorthold
    Tenancy Agreements 73
  furnished 66–7, 69
    inventories 76
  gas and electricity safety certificates
    70–1
  Housing Associations 65
  leaving 79
  letting/estate agencies 66
  local council 66
  location 69, 70
  lodgers 64
  moving in 76–7
  private landlords 64–5
  references 72
  rent payments 73, 75, 76–7

repairs and maintenance 74
reporting damage 79
student accommodation 78
sub-letting 65
tenancy agreements 65, 69, 73–5
things to find out before viewing 69–70
viewing 70–1
see also landlords; shared accommodation
resuscitation *see* CPR
rice, and food poisoning 167
rights
arrests 278
employees 242–3
tenants 74–5
Rohypnol 254, 255
Roofie Foundation 256
roofs, water coming through 322

S

safety
electric drills 118
food 162–8
frozen food 158–9
in the home 135–8
microwaves 161
and Internet banking 19
see also personal safety
salads, pre-packed 140
salt, and stain removal 105
Samaritans 200
satinwood paint 122
saucepans
fires 316
non-stick 148, 154
sauces 178
saving money
cheap eating 174–5
cutting expenses 52–4
free dental treatment 224–5
free eye checks 226
savings accounts 27, 43
scams 56–7
Scottish legal system 265
screwdrivers 109
screws 109, 115
in hollow plasterboard walls 115, 116
in solid plaster walls 115–16
where not to put 117

security *see* home security; personal safety
security alarms 257
self-defence classes 258
self-employment, starting your own business 241
self-help books 227
sex
and alcohol 250, 254
drug rape 254–6
sexual health 200
sexually transmitted diseases (STDs) 200, 256
shared accommodation 69
agreeing ground rules 85
Houses in Multiple Occupation (HMOs) 64–5, 82
paying for food 83
problems with 85–6
sheets 103–4, 107
Shelter 80, 87, 319
shock
and burns 290
and fractures/dislocations 297
and head injuries 298
signs and treatment of 305
shopping, cutting expenses 52–3
showers
descaling 120
filling cracks beside edges 121
removing mildew from edges 120
unblocking 119
sick people, exposure to 187–8
sickness/diarrhoea/food poisoning 215–17
silk emulsion 121
sinks
filling cracks beside edges 121
removing mildew from edges 120
unblocking 119
sleep, poor patterns of 229
slugs 131
smear tests 196, 197
smiling 187
smoke detectors 136
smoking 136, 139
social life 228
soda water, and stain removal 105
soft-sheen emulsion 122
solicitors, and arrests 277, 278
spectacles 226
spinal injuries 309

spirits, units of 251–2
Spotless 94–5
spray polishes 101
stain removal 104–6
 and bleach 102–3, 104–5
 blood stains 106
 carpets, sofas and clothing 104–6
 chocolate stains 106
 coffee stains 106
 and vinegar 106
 wine stains 105–6
standing orders 36–7
 for rent payments 77
STDs (sexually transmitted diseases)
 200, 256
stir-fries 173, 178
store cards 29, 30
stress 187, 227–30
 breathing and relaxation 228–9
student accommodation officers 78, 87
students
 and council tax 83
 and crime prevention 257, 258
 student accommodation 78, 93
 support systems for 245
students' unions 245, 321
study 245
 keeping on top of things 245
 and stress 227–8
sunlight 186
supermarkets, and cheap eating 174, 175

T

taps
 dripping 127
 mains taps 125–7
taxation 42–4
 council tax 67, 82–3
 and credit rating 41
 evasion or avoidance 43
 on interest payments 24, 26, 27, 43,
 44
 P60/P45 forms 243
 and PAYE (Pay as You Earn) 42, 43
 personal allowance 42
 tax returns 43–4
 VAT (Value Added Tax) 133
tea tree oil 213
teeth 224–5
telephone banking services 18
telephone bills 81

Telephone Preference Service 57
telephones
 payphones 81
 tariffs 52
 see also mobile phones
television licences 82
temperature, taking your 209
temping 240–1
tenancy agreements 65, 69, 73–5
 Assured Tenancies 73, 74
 duties as a tenant 75
 fixed term Assured Shorthold
  Tenancy Agreements 73
 rights as a tenant 74–5
tetanus vaccinations 197
theft 257–9
 emergencies 312, 320–1
throat infections 214
thunder storms, and electrical
 equipment 138
toasters 137
toilets 128–9
 blocked 128
 constantly flushing 128–9
tonsillitis 214
tools for DIY 109
tourists, and crime 260–1
toxic shock syndrome 208
tradespeople 132–4
 call-out charges 132
 CORGI-registered 132, 137
 electricians 133
 emergency 132
 finding 141
 guarantees 133
 paying 133–4
 plumbers 119, 129, 130, 132, 133,
  322
 and VAT 133
Trading Standards Office 133–4, 273
travel insurance 31, 46, 48–9, 261
travelling abroad 260–1
Troubleshoot sections 9
 accommodation 87
 food 179
 health 231
 household repairs 141
 the law 279
 money 59
 personal safety 262
 work 246
tumble-dryers 98–9

U

unconsciousness 207, 208, 222
 choking 292–3
 and CPR 306–8
 diabetes 294
 electric shock 295
 fractures/dislocation 297
 head injuries 298
 poisoning 303
Unemployment Benefits *see* Jobseeker's
 Allowance
unfurnished accommodation 66, 69
university accommodation 78, 87, 93
utility bills 81–2, 84

V

vaccinations 188, 197
 flu 188
vacuum cleaners 103
VAT (Value Added Tax) 133
Vegan Society 172, 179
vegans 172
vegetables 172–3, 186
 frozen 156
Vegetarian Society 171, 179
vegetarians 170–1
Victim Support 259
victims of crime 257–9
 burglaries 253
 crime prevention 257–8
 emergencies 312
 muggings 253
 reporting crime 258–9
vinegar
 as a descaler 120
 and stain removal 106
viruses 215
Visa cards 29
visas 261
vitamin supplements 188–9
vitamins 170, 171

W

Walk-In Injury Clinic 206
wall plugs 115, 116
wallet, loss of 320–1
wallpaper
 painting over 122
 removing 122

walls
 drilling into 117
 screws in
  hollow plasterboard walls 115, 116
  solid plaster walls 115–16
washing machines
 laundry symbols and instructions
  96–7
 washing power/liquid 97–8
wasps 131
water 125–30
 airlocks in radiators 128
 burst pipes 125, 126–7
 coming through a ceiling/roof 322
 dripping taps 127
 finding pipes in walls 117
 leaks 127, 322
 mains taps 125–7
 meters 81, 129
 outlets 127
 preventing frozen pipes 129–30
 servicing the boiler 132
 toilets 128–9
water-rates 81–2
welfare benefits *see* benefits (state)
wheat-free diets 172
window locks 77
wine
 stains 105–6
 units of 251
wood
 cleaning 101
 screws in 115
work 235, 236–44
 employee rights 242–3
 getting work 236–41
  CVs 236, 237, 238–9
  interviews 236–7, 239–40
 keeping your job 244
 starting your own business 241
 and state benefits 240
 and stress 227–8
 temping 240–1
 Troubleshoot 246
 see also taxation
Working Families Tax Credit 194, 240
wounds, first aid for 222

INDEX